The Role of Service- Learning in Educational Reform

by Robert Bhaerman,
Karin Cordell, and Barbara Gomez

National Society for Experiential Education

SIMON & SCHUSTER CUSTOM PUBLISHING

Library of Congress Catalog Number 97-067379

Printed in the United States of America

10 9 8 7 6 5 4 3 2 1

This book was provided camera ready by the author.

Please visit our website at www.sscp.com

ISBN 0-536-01028-5

BA 98013

 SIMON & SCHUSTER CUSTOM PUBLISHING
160 Gould Street/Needham Heights, MA 02194
Simon & Schuster Education Group

If we do not lay out ourselves in the service of mankind, whom should we serve?

· ·

— Abigail Adams

NSEE is pleased to publish *The Role of Service-Learning in Educational Reform*, a comprehensive monograph that describes the linkages between service-learning and educational reform. In this monograph, service-learning is not seen as an end in itself, but rather, a method of teaching and learning which involves many of the same elements comprising school reform.

Assessing the effectiveness of our work in the educational arena has become more critical than ever. Everyone from practitioners to policymakers is being held more accountable for their work. The increasing emphasis on goals, and more particularly the outcomes of goals, is clearly evident at all educational levels.

The Role of Service-Learning in Educational Reform challenges each of us to step outside of our particular niches and actively seek methods for connecting our work to other initiatives in education. We must ask ourselves how what we want to achieve relates to parallel or larger ventures. It is precisely through these intersections and linkages that we can accomplish multiple goals collaboratively. In fact, the authors of the monograph argue that for service-learning to reach its full potential, its relationship with systemic reform must be recognized and pursued.

NSEE believes that some of the broader objectives of integrating experience and learning — civic responsibility, workforce preparation, and respect for diversity — lie at the heart of educational reform. This assertion is congruent with the work of NSEE — an organization that fosters the effective use of experience as an integral part of learning. We invite you to explore the possibilities that exist for deeper and more meaningful outcomes in your work as you read *The Role of Service-Learning in Educational Reform*.

Sally Migliore
Executive Director

National Society for Experiential Education

. . . .

Acknowledgments

The authors are deeply indebted to the many individuals, state service-learning coordinators, and organizations who submitted detailed program descriptions, evaluation reports, and resource materials that were extremely useful in preparing this monograph — all of whom are cited in the appendices. Special thanks also is extended to John Connolly, Director, and Dick Corbett, former Co-Director of the Applied Research Unit, of Research for Better Schools, Inc., who provided valuable reviews of the first draft of this monograph.

Table of Contents

The primary purpose of this monograph is to illustrate how community service-learning is one vehicle for achieving the goals of education and youth development, and concurrently, how it is highly consistent with the goals of "systemic educational reform." The intended audiences are policymakers at all levels who are seeking effective educational policies and programs for accomplishing both education and social reform, local administrators who are attempting to make decisions regarding their degree of support for service-learning, and teachers and coordinators of service-learning initiatives who are becoming more involved in relevant policy decisions that often have a direct effect on the school environment and the curriculum. Throughout the narrative, we purposely have not referred to service-learning as a "program," but rather as an instructional strategy, a philosophy, and a process. The term "program" implies that service-learning in itself is the end goal or product. As we will attempt to explain, service-learning is much more than that. The monograph focuses on a series of eight questions relating to what we know about service-learning and seven questions relating to how service-learning links to and supports school improvement and reform efforts.

The first series of questions deals with the following topics: the *definition* of service-learning as a method of teaching and learning; the *need* for service-learning, including a brief historical overview and rationale; the *types* of service-learning as viewed from various perspectives; examples of how service-learning is integrated into *curricula* at various levels from early elementary school to high school; and an exploration of the nature of service-learning *instruction,* including the concept of reflection and the issue of student assessment.

Other questions relate to the major *barriers* to integrating service-learning into curriculum and instruction, as well as several important legal concerns; the *purported benefits and results* of service-learning, including quantitative and qualitative research findings; and a number of *relevant issues* that must be addressed.

The second series of questions, on the linkage of service-learning with school reform efforts, addresses the following topics: the *definitions* of "systemic educational reform" from the perspectives of several educators; the *linkages* between service-learning and the GOALS 2000: Educate America Act, the Improving America's Schools Act of 1994, and the School-to-Work Opportunities Act; state support of service-learning in relation to *state educational reform initiatives*; and the *visions* of several educators regarding service-learning as a component of school reform. The second series of questions also includes a brief summary and comparison of the following components of both "systemic educational reform" and service-learning: visions of a new educational system; public and political support; networking with partners; teaching and learning changes; administrative roles and responsibilities; and policymaking and policy alignment.

The monograph is based on the realization that for service-learning to be a lasting part of education, it must be viewed as a philosophy, a process, and an instructional strategy rather than an interrupting or intrusive program or project. As a method of teaching and learning, it provides a real audience and purpose for learning, an excellent entry point to learning styles, and an opportunity for the application of academic concepts through experience and reflection. Moreover, it should never become a burden that teachers are forced to incorporate into their professional responsibilities.

The monograph concludes that both service-learning and "systemic educational reform" are based on and share 12 common principles relating to:

- policy and program alignment;
- standards;
- school social systems and community connections;
- school/community partnerships;
- building respect and tolerance;
- the school's culture and governance structure;
- higher-order thinking, decision-making, and problem-solving skills;
- the application of knowledge;
- the integration of curriculum, instruction, and assessment;
- the integration of academic and applied learning;
- the active engagement of life-long learners; and
- authentic ways of ascertaining what students know and can do.

Service-learning, in short, can be a way of recapturing the idealism of the 1960s but with "value added," i.e., with a strong learning component complementing an equally strong service ethic. But whether a service-learning culture permeates schools and communities or remains on the fringes of the educational reform agenda is still unknown. Its considerable potential for educational revitalization, however, is beyond question.

Part I

What Do We Know about Service-Learning?

. . . .

What Exactly Is Service-Learning?

The Alliance for Service-Learning in Education Reform (1993) defined service-learning as a method of teaching and learning:

- by which young people learn and develop through active participation in thoughtfully organized service experiences that meet community needs and that are coordinated in collaboration with the school and community;

- that is integrated into the academic curriculum or provides structured time for a young person to think, talk, or write about what he/she did and saw during the service activity;

- that provides young people with opportunities to use newly acquired academic skills and knowledge in real-life situations in their own communities; and

- that enhances what is taught in the school by extending student learning beyond the classroom and into the community and helps to foster the development of a sense of caring for others. (71)

The major components of the concept are embodied in the definition, namely, active student participation, thoughtfully organized experiences, focus on community needs and school/community coordination, academic curriculum integration, structured time for reflection, opportunities for application of skills and knowledge, extended learning opportunities, and development of a sense of caring for others. Service-learning, in short, provides a holistic, constructivist vision of the learning process and is based on what we know about how students best learn.

Because service-learning initiatives have been increasing rapidly during the past decade, accurate current data on their exact number is difficult to verify. Data from the mid-1980s indicate that approximately 27 percent (i.e., 5,400) of the high schools in this country offered some type of community service (Conrad and Hedin, 1989). With the passage of the National and Community Service Act of 1990 and the National and Community Service Trust Act of 1993, there has been a significant increase in school-based community service and service-learning at the K–12 level throughout the decade. In academic year 1994–95 alone, nearly 700,000 elementary, middle, and high school students were involved in service-learning activities through programs supported by the Corporation for National Service. This figure does not reflect the thousands of students involved in service-learning as part of privately supported national initiatives or in non-public schools.

. . . .

Because the concept has several dimensions, advocates have come to view service-learning through a variety of perspectives. For example, service-learning has been viewed as a way of learning and a vision of youth (Cairn, 1992); a point of view and ethic (Briscoe, 1991); and a curricular tool (Smilow, 1993). McPherson (Northwest Regional Education Laboratory, 1994) explains that service-learning and community service are not synonymous:

> ... (there is) a distinction between service learning as a pedagogy or a way of teaching as opposed to community service as a way of fostering an ethic of volunteerism and participation. Service learning is a way of helping make the content learning more engaging. ... It is a direct link to what they're learning in the classroom, and it's really a way of demonstrating that they understand the concepts. (4–5)

Shaffer (1993) views service-learning as a "nexus" between community service and experiential education in that it engages students in meaningful service by facilitating the experiences from which academic learnings are derived. The service activities, he suggests, advance the ethic of civic responsibility by developing more caring and compassionate individuals who — as students — make meaningful contributions to their communities. Service-learning creates opportunities for students to connect to community issues since they would assume a portion of the responsibility for the well-being of their communities. Engaging students in meaningful service sends a message that they are needed.

Shaffer also contends that service-learning echoes John Dewey's emphasis on active student participation and community involvement in the educational process. Such initiatives motivate learning since students become actively engaged in the process and develop their content skills. By combining civic responsibility and experiential education, service-learning becomes a powerful tool through which academic and social objectives of education can be accomplished.

These visions can be traced, in part, to the broad view which President Clinton holds on the concept of community service:

> ... To see an America where service is a way of life. ... I think of schools where young people are called not only to academic achievement but to volunteer work in hospitals and nursing homes, tutoring programs, and homeless shelters as a fundamental component of education. (Corporation for National and Community Service, 1993, 3)

The term "service-learning" (with and without the hyphen) increasingly has appeared in the recent educational literature, reflecting the fact that the concept has emerged as a popular educational strategy. Does it matter that sometimes a hyphen is used to connect the two words and sometimes it is not? Perhaps it does. The hyphen implies that a two-way street exists, that is *service is enhanced though learning and learning is enhanced through service*. The two words are inseparable. It is not a question of one word modifying the other. Both are of equal value and, hence, should be connected to illustrate their unbreakable linkage.

· ·

Why Is Service-Learning Needed?

A Brief Historical Overview

The roots of service-learning can be traced, in part, to the depression years when President Franklin Roosevelt created the Civilian Conservation Corps through which thousands of unemployed young people found work as well as a sense of well-being. More recently, the legacies of President John Kennedy continue in the Peace Corps and the Volunteers in Service to America (VISTA).

Legislators have continued to support the ideas of youth service by establishing the National Student Volunteer Program in the early 1970s, a division of VISTA that encouraged school-based service by means of conferences, workshops, a quarterly journal, and a small grant program (Shaffer, 1993). Shaffer suggests that various reports during this period (e.g., the National Committee on Secondary Education in 1972, the Panel on Youth of the President's Science Advisory Committee in 1974, and the National Panel on High School and Adolescent Education in 1976) each embraced community service as a means of bridging the gap between adolescence and adulthood.

Conrad and Hedin (1989), who have traced the concept in the educational literature, report that recommendations for service to be part of schooling have appeared in recurring cycles since the early 1900s as well as in recent educational reform proposals. They look back at the relevancy of John Dewey's ideas on how learning takes place, at William Kilpatrick's unit method in which learning occurs in settings both inside and outside of the school, at George County's belief that schools should inculcate the values of social democracy, and at the mid-1950's Citizenship Education Project at Columbia University's Teachers College that, among other things, stressed community participation and learning.

Discussions of service-learning also appear in recent educational writings. Conrad and Hedin cite the work of such educators as Eliot Wigginton, whose *Sometimes A Shining Moment* describes Foxfire projects that offer inspiration and practical assistance to teachers working with youth services; John Goodlad, whose *A Place Called School* includes community service among the strategies to improve education; and Ernest Boyer, whose book, *High School*, recommends that schools require 120 hours of community

· ·

service for graduation. They also cite the widely reported W.T. Grant Foundation's *The Forgotten Half* (published in 1988) that makes a strong plea for community service by non-college-bound youth and argues for creating quality service opportunities as fundamental in all schools in this country.

Lastly, Conrad and Hedin review the involvement of a number of organizations that assist educators in planning and implementing service-learning, e.g., the National Society for Experiential Education, the Council of Chief State School Officers, the Education Commission of the States, and the National Association of Secondary School Principals. These organizations — and many others — view the potential of service-learning as one way of addressing the massive social problems that youth confront as we move closer to the year 2000.

A Rationale

Senator Kennedy (1991) stated that "in quieter times" Americans always served their communities by helping neighbors in need and strangers in trouble. But who needs to be reminded that American citizens in the 1990s are living through anything but "quieter times"? More often than not, the "neighbors in need" are our own.

There are many reasons for including service-learning in our schools. As Perrone (1993) suggests, society faces an assortment of problems: a youth culture that has few connections to civic life, feelings among youth of having no vital place in society, deteriorating communities, and an increased pessimism about the future. Other observers see much of the same. They see youth as passive observers rather than active participants in community life (Shaffer, 1993); they see the growing alienation of youth (Schine, 1989); and they see many youth suffering from isolation, boredom, the lack of family structure, deep poverty, easy access to alcohol and drugs, the proliferation of weapons, and intense pressure to be sexually active (Orenstein, 1992). In a society that generally values one's importance by one's job, many adolescents are seen as non-contributing members of society (Alliance for Service-Learning in Education Reform, 1993).

But many also see hope. They see service-learning as a powerful tool that could transform young people from passive recipients to active providers and, in doing so, change the perception of youth from a cause of many problems to a source of many solutions (Alliance for Service-Learning in Education Reform, 1993); they see involvement in community as a means of rejuvenating the ethic of civic responsibility (Shaffer, 1993); and they see service as a way of stimulating learning and social development, preserving democracy, and serving as an antidote to the alienation and separation of youth from the community (Conrad and Hedin, 1989).

Schine (1989) senses that, although the primary reason for involving adolescents in community service is to provide opportunities to assume meaningful roles (including leadership roles), service-learning has several other components including those that reside in the changing nature of communities. Traditionally, she suggests, we have depended on volunteers for a wide range of services and for creative solutions to community problems. Schine sees the need for such services continuing unabated and likely increasing as greater numbers of the very young and old now require services that once were provided by families.

Schine also presents a strong case for expanding opportunities for adolescents to contribute to their communities. She bases this position on the awareness of the unique needs and traits of the 11-to-14-year old. Early adolescence, she notes, is characterized primarily by change, not only the most obvious physical ones but also cognitive and emotional changes. This is a time when attachments to parents are loosened and ties to peers are intensified. The changes include the shift from periods of extreme self-doubt and unpredictable changes in mood — all normal developmental shifts. During this period, there also is a dawning of idealism and altruism that at times may seem to be at odds with adolescents' self-absorbed behaviors. The desire to relate to adults other than parents and teachers, to test values, and to try new roles are important characteristics of this age group.

According to research conducted by Schine (1989), service-learning can meet many of the needs of early adolescent youth: developing a sense of competency and discovering new skills; discovering a place for themselves in the world; creating a vision of a personal future; participating in activities with tangible outcomes; knowing a variety of adults from different backgrounds, including potential role models; having freedom to take part in the world of adults but also to be free to retreat to a world of their peers; testing a developing value system in authentic situations; speaking, being heard, and knowing they can make a difference; achieving recognition for their accomplishments and having opportunities to make real decisions within appropriate limits; and receiving support and guidance from adults who appreciate their problems and their promise.

As Schine (1989) notes, general agreement exists among those who work with adolescents that one of the most meaningful roles for this age group involves interpersonal relationships. Youth volunteers who work with the very young or old often receive a warm welcome and affection and, at the same time, enhance their own self-esteem by realizing they are valued and they do make a difference. She also contends that the rationale for service-learning is incomplete without noting the debate surrounding "character education." While many people agree that the public school should stress citizenship education, less agreement exists regarding the teaching of values. Schine cites a Baltimore County task force report that identifies values that can and should be taught in schools, e.g., compassion, courtesy, equality of opportunity, regard for human worth and dignity, and respecting the rights of others. She concludes that nothing could be more effective in reinforcing these values than enacting them.

Other relevant insights on adolescent development have been presented by the Carnegie Council on Adolescent Development (1990). Several states have been involved, through a grant program by the Carnegie Corporation of New York, in implementing the Council's recommendations for transforming education for young adolescents. The recommendations, based on the developmental needs of adolescents, focus on opportunities for youth service. In the area of connecting schools with communities, the Council recommends that opportunities for youth service be provided under the auspices of schools collaborating with community agencies.

Much of the literature on the prevention of high-risk behaviors addresses key elements of service-learning. Benard (1990), in particular, sees youth participation in meaningful community tasks as a critical factor in prevention in that it heightens self-esteem and enhances moral development. The antithesis of participation, Benard argues, is further alienation from and lack of social bonding with such major socializing institutions as the family, school, and community. She concludes that although youth service opportunities must be a central component of comprehensive prevention programming, to date they have not received the attention in prevention policy that they deserve. Kurth-Schai (1988) similarly maintains that since many educational policies and practices are based on the view of youth as problems rather than resources, many prevention policies and practices also reflect this point of view.

While many of the previous points focus on individual character development, other arguments relate to broader issues of civic responsibility, the promotion of democratic values, and patterns of responsible social behavior. Seigel and Rockwood (1993) hold that participant involvement in social action means more than simply making a difference in a community, but rather creating lasting changes that, in turn, will make a difference, i.e., socially responsible citizens often become more empowered as they exercise social action. Seigel and Rockwood conclude that social responsibility requires developing a social consciousness and such values as caring, respecting, sharing, learning to think critically, empathizing with another person's perspectives, and connecting with the larger community by taking action on important social issues. Similarly, Sagawa and Halperin (1993) support the position (attributed to Benjamin Barber) that service is an indispensable prerequisite of citizenship and a condition for the preservation of democracy.

Boyte (1991), who further establishes a bond between service-learning and civic education, however, does not see a sufficiently strong emphasis on connecting students' everyday concerns with the political process. He submits that the majority of service-learning efforts spend too little time addressing the policy dimensions of issues and typically leave little room for political learning. Boyte recommends, from the perspective of civil education, that the community service conception be considerably broadened.

In short, various rationales support the implementation of service-learning. Some emphasize the benefits to adolescents; others have a broader perspective and advocate — as do the authors of this monograph — service-learning from K to 12 and beyond. Some focus on youth development theory; others on prevention theory; some on the issues of social and civic responsibility; and others on both dimensions, i.e., youth development and civic responsibility. Still others stress the applications of academic learning, i.e., making learning more relevant, more meaningful, and longer lasting. Lastly, others stress the relevance of service-learning to career exploration.

The advocates of service-learning, Haberman (1994) observes, are a "hardy band of reformers" who attempt to address a multitude of individual and social needs. Haberman, whose keen insights always cut to the heart of the matter, maintains that these advocates rightfully contend that young people without connectedness and commitment to their communities are victims of a less-than-equal education.

. . . .

What Are the Types of Service-Learning?

E ffective service-learning responds to both the developmental/learning needs of youth and the social/cultural needs of communities. The Alliance for Service-Learning in Education Reform (1993) recommends service-learning initiatives that reflect the maturity and capacities of youth at different stages; the duration of service role, desired outcomes, structure for reflection, and, particularly, the types of services must be age-appropriate.

The State of Maryland's Approach

In 1990, through action by the State Board of Education, Maryland became the first state to require community service for high school graduation. The requirement, which first applied to the graduating class of 1995, states that each student shall complete 75 hours of service that includes preparation, action, and reflection. At the discretion of the local district, activities can start in the middle grades. An option is participation in a locally designed initiative approved by the state superintendent (Maryland State Department of Education, n.d.). The state education agency has identified three distinct activities — direct service, indirect service, and advocacy — each distinguished by who is served, how they are served, and by what students learn.

Direct service   These activities place students face-to-face in helping someone, e.g., peer and cross-age tutoring, mentoring, and visiting the elderly. Students who are at risk of failing and those with low self-esteem often benefit from performing direct service. Such service usually occurs weekly for several weeks or months and is enhanced when students have prior training. It also helps if the people they are serving know about the students before they arrive. Since students often work with people different from themselves, the experiences help them overcome fears and biases they may have about others.

Indirect service   Activities are performed "behind the scenes" by channeling resources to alleviate a problem, i.e., students may not even come into contact with those they serve. In some cases, the activities benefit the community as a whole rather than a particular group. Some examples are environmental projects such as planting trees and cleaning stream beds, conducting food and clothing drives, building ramps and installing door latches

. . . .

for independent-living senior citizens, and conducting clean-up projects. Indirect service activities, characteristically undertaken by large groups, often are annual or one-time special events involving a great deal of planning but little reflection. They are popular because they do not interrupt the schedule or, if they do, they interrupt everyone's schedule at the same time. These projects tend to be least valuable since students may not actually see the benefit of their efforts first hand.

Advocacy   Students engaged in advocacy often lend their voices and talents to aid the disenfranchised or to correct perceived injustices. Once students have helped an individual, they may perform other initiatives to eliminate the causes of the problem or inform the public about the issue. Such activities include lobbying public officials to take a new course of action, petitioning, making presentations, and conducting community surveys and presenting the results. They also might undertake such consciousness-raising activities as distributing literature and involving others in service. Students at Wicomico High School in Maryland, for example, led a "Disability Week" including sensitivity training that allowed participants to experience simulated speech, hearing, and vision impairments.

[NOTE: The use of these descriptive categories appears to be catching on since other state agencies are beginning to describe their initiatives in terms of direct service, indirect service, and advocacy, e.g., the South Carolina Department of Education (1994.)]

The Council of Chief State School Officers' Analysis

The Council of Chief State School Officers (1994) has developed a five-item continuum of service-learning ranging from low to high curriculum infusion. The dimensions, from the lowest to highest infusion, are briefly described below.

Community service classes   Students spend a portion of the week — usually four days of class time — performing service. The fifth day is devoted to training, reflecting, evaluating, and other group activities. The services normally include tutoring, mentoring, peer counseling, and providing companionship. Courses typically are offered for elective credit or for academic credit as a substitute for language arts or social studies requirements. The focus is primarily to learn about community service and is not connected to academic content area(s).

Community projects   Students demonstrate their academic knowledge and skills through involvement in long-term projects as part of course work or performance assessment. Supervision and evaluation usually occur under the guidance of faculty, parents, and/or community members.

Schoolwide themes   Grades, schools, or entire districts select a theme that is carried out across classes and grade levels. This approach often facilitates interdisciplinary teaching, cooperative learning, and developing students' leadership skills.

Instructional method in core curriculum   An intensive group project serves as the experience around which skills are developed, either in one or several academic areas. This approach is essential to institutionalizing restructured teaching/learning environments that foster higher-order thinking, problem-solving skills, and enhanced student achievement.

Schoolwide infusion   The infusion of service-learning can be viewed in three ways: As an instructional strategy or *pedagogy* that involves youth as important community resources; as a *philosophy* that encourages the creation of a caring community of learners who strive to improve the school's culture and governance; and/or a *process* that facilitates a community-wide strategy to improve both the quality of education and life in a community.

Conrad and Hedin's Analysis

Conrad and Hedin (1989) distinguish five types of service-learning initiatives with regard to how closely they are integrated into the school's schedule.

Special events and co-curricular activities   These events and activities are common in all high schools, e.g., students bring imperishable food for the needy, conduct neighborhood clean-ups, and the like. The activities often are conducted under the auspices of a student council or club. It is estimated that students average about one hour per week in service activities for which they receive no academic credit. The nature of clubs varies greatly. Some have service as a central activity; others, such as the National Honor Society, include service as one obligation of membership. Some clubs are branches of such national service organizations as the Key Club affiliated with Kiwanis. Typically a faculty advisor — sometimes paid, sometimes a volunteer —guides the students. Conrad and Hedin indicate that this approach may be the purest form of service since activities are strictly voluntary. The students usually receive no academic credit or time off and are responsible for a significant leadership role. However, such activities may lack tangible incentives beyond the intrinsic value of serving and may lead to involving primarily those students who already possess a service ethic and excluding others who could profit from such service. Examples include students visiting nursing homes, working at soup kitchens, conducting clothing or blood drives, and participating in voter registration campaigns.

Service credit or requirements   In some schools, elective credit is awarded for an established number of hours (e.g., 100 hours equals one semester credit). In other cases, students are required to perform a specified number of hours of service in order to graduate. A common practice is for a student to prepare a detailed plan for a proposed activity. The plan is reviewed by a faculty advisor or project coordinator who also certifies that the activity has been completed. Although this approach is essentially an independent activity with minimal staff supervision, there may be occasional discussions with advisors.

Laboratories for an existing course   Students perform services as a way to gather, test, and apply the content and skills of existing courses, e.g., students in a contemporary social issues class may gain insights into a problem by helping to alleviate it; language students may test and expand their skills by teaching younger students. The service, either a one-time activity or an ongoing commitment, may be done for extra credit or as a course requirement. According to Conrad and Hedin, this type of integration enables schools to introduce community service into academic programs with relatively little or no change in the basic curriculum, schedule, or staff development. An example would be students receiving points toward their social studies grade for volunteering up to 20 hours per quarter.

Community service classes   Such classes feature the interchange of action and reflection in courses that are integral to the academic program. Their primary characteristic is that service, the central activity, is undertaken both for its own sake and for stimulating classroom experiences. The emphasis is on providing information and skills and generalizing principles to help students learn from their experiences as well as to work more effectively in their service assignments. For example, students in a social studies class might be in the community four days a week and in class one day. An additional class period is gained at no extra cost by providing double course credit and by counting the course as two classes for the teacher; a two-period block gives students sufficient time to be involved significantly in their assignments without infringing on the rest of their school schedule.

One example is the "Community Action Program" at John Marshall High School in Rochester, Minnesota, where students meet their 12th-grade requirement through a two-period class that weaves together service and reflection. Students volunteer three days in a variety of agencies and special-need programs in schools; they remain in school one day to discuss their experiences, work on helping skills, and relate social studies concepts to their work with people; during the remaining day, they usually visit agencies to learn about programs first hand. In "English as a Second Language (ESL) Peer Tutoring" at Hopkins High School in Minnetonka, Minnesota, the ESL peer tutoring class pairs native-born students with immigrant students — mainly from Southeast Asia — for one class period daily. Usually there is both a morning and afternoon session, and both students who tutor and those who are tutored schedule this as any other class and receive the same elective credit. At the beginning of the semester, tutors are given extensive orientation into the cultural background of the students with whom they will work as well as guidance on what and how to teach.

Service as a schoolwide or K–12 focus   School-wide and K–12 efforts are a relatively under-developed approach. At the school level, each department determines how the knowledge and skills of its discipline can be applied for the betterment of the community (e.g., child development students assisting in a nursery school, technology education students offering home repairs to the poor, English students reading to and writing letters for nursing home residents, and mathematics students providing computer services to nonprofit agencies). Students in the school serve as cross-age tutors at every grade level. As Conrad and Hedin suggest, the schoolwide approach carries the "laboratory" concept into all aspects of the curriculum; the K–12 focus extends the approach vertically as well as horizontally and with increasing complexity. Service-learning, therefore, is not an isolated event for a few highly motivated students but an integral part of the school experience for all.

Although the integrated approach has not been widely practiced at this point, several examples exist. For example, "Student Service-Learning" in The Tucson Unified School District has established a partnership with the Puma Council on Aging. Schools at all levels are encouraged to provide age-appropriate services to senior citizens, e.g., elementary school classes participate in pen pal, adopt-a-senior, and Grandparents Day programs; middle and high school students clean yards and wash windows — and at the same time develop caring relationships with their senior neighbors. "Community Service-Learning" in Springfield, Massachusetts, established a position of District Coordinator for Community Service-Learning along with a building representative and service-learning team in each school. Their job is to develop and integrate themes and age-appropriate activities into the curriculum. In the elementary school, the goal is to integrate such themes as hunger and homelessness; in the middle schools, each building has activities tied to such content as environmental action projects in science; and, at the high school level, an elective course, "We Make A Difference," was established along with making community service a frequent theme in writing assignments.

Cairn's Analysis

Cairn (1992, 22–23) describes five types of strategies for developing learner outcomes. Since the strategies *describe* rather than *prescribe* structures, Cairn cautions that no one strategy should be taken as the recommended model. Nor are the strategies prioritized since, in any given situation, each has unique advantages and disadvantages. Each strategy includes reflection; adequate orientation and training; and the involvement of teachers, students, and community representatives. The five types — including teacher and student roles, possible learner outcomes, and strengths and weaknesses — are summarized below.

Youth as volunteers: service as experiential education — one-time group projects, e.g., visits to a nursing home, paint-a-thons, or individual placements in volunteer positions.

- *Teacher and student roles:* conducting community needs assessments, selecting services that address identified needs, and identifying skills to be learned.

- *Possible learner outcomes:* increased self-esteem, social responsibility, cooperation, communication skills, experience with diversity, exposure to careers and knowledge and skills needed to complete the service.

- *Strengths/weaknesses:* The strategy is useful as an extension of the curriculum but is not a particularly strong instructional method. Although the main lesson is that young people can make a contribution, it does not challenge them intellectually as do other strategies.

Community as laboratory for learning: service-learning as experiential education — one-time group projects or individual placements in existing volunteer positions.

- *Teacher and student roles:* conducting both learner and community needs assessments, selecting services that address identified needs, and identifying skills to be learned.

- *Possible learner outcomes:* same as above, plus writing, computation, vocabulary, public speaking, and understanding personal relationships.

- *Strengths/weaknesses:* The strategy offers learners opportunities to understand the relevance of what they are learning and to improve their ability to serve. Because service sites usually are established by teachers, students get less organizational experience developing activities than in the following strategies.

Community as proving ground: service-learning as assessment — one-time group or individual projects.

- *Teachers and student roles:* conducting learner needs assessments; also, teachers help students gain knowledge and skills using traditional classroom activities. Students test mastery of knowledge and skills in meeting community needs; teachers help students strengthen areas of weakness or gain new knowledge and skills.

- *Possible learner outcomes:* emphasizes the use of service-learning as a means of assessing learning.

- *Strengths/weaknesses:* Students have an opportunity to apply theory in real life practice. Because service only occurs at the end of the learning process, this strategy provides less opportunity for students to learn from the experience and bring those learnings back to the classroom.

Community/school partnership for service and learning: service-learning as the engine for learning — extended group or individual projects.

- *Teachers and student roles:* conducting learner and community needs assessments, developing student skill and knowledge inventories, establishing learning objectives based on skills and information needed to complete activities, and participating in curriculum planning based on learner and community needs.

- *Possible learner outcomes:* same as the first and third strategies, plus self-understanding, appreciation of diversity, motivation to learn, critical thinking, leadership skills, understanding career options, and the ability to apply and adapt academic skills in work and life settings.

- *Strengths/weaknesses:* The strategy can lead to the achievement of strong outcomes that evolve with progressive learner achievements. Learners are motivated by the real needs of others; teachers must be comfortable involving and empowering learners.

Combination of strategies: service-learning as an integrated strategy

- *Teacher and student roles:* identifying both learner and community needs and desired outcomes; teachers need to make certain that students play a central role in decision making.

- *Possible learner outcomes:* same as those listed above.

- *Strengths/weaknesses:* Service-learning is not a subject in itself, but rather it is partly an educational methodology, partly a philosophy of learning, and partly a developmental strategy for schools and communities. Because strategies are based on both community and learner needs, they require great flexibility and work best as a complement to other reform initiatives.

Duckenfield and Swanson's Analysis

Service-learning can be integrated into the curriculum through a series of progressively complex levels of implementation. According to Duckenfield and Swanson (1992), schools should introduce activities at the most basic level and gradually advance to higher ones as the students experience success.

Level one: extracurricular Activities are voluntary; students do not receive credit or time off from school. One example is a volunteer clearinghouse staffed by students and faculty that provides information on community service opportunities. However, such activities rarely include opportunities for reflection about or connection to the students' school experiences.

Level two: curricular unit Teachers introduce service-learning without involving new courses or staff, e.g., a service-learning unit offered through a regular course. Such a unit helps fulfill the academic goals of the course. Another option is independent study in which students serve outside regular classroom hours but receive academic credit.

Level three: mandatory or elective courses Service-learning is a regular class in the school's program. Although it can be an integral part of any academic area, the most natural place is in social studies where courses combine service experiences with classroom experiences. The classroom provides skills to assist students in interpreting their experiences and operating successfully in their placement.

Level four: schoolwide integration The highest level of implementation is service as a schoolwide theme. One variation is a community service focus in an entire school or district where service to others is woven into many courses and serves as an organizing principle for the total academic program. The school, in effect, is organized to serve the community, since the curriculum centers on addressing community issues. This level has the potential to reach all students rather than only a few motivated one.

Schine's Analysis

Schine (1989) distinguishes between school-based and community-based efforts. The term, "school-based," however, has various connotations; e.g., to the Corporation for National Service, school-based efforts mean that the schools initiate and administer the grants and activities. The connotation in Schine's perspective is that service-learning activities actually take place *within* the school.

School-based   School-based initiatives offer several advantages in that they circumvent the need for transportation and alleviate communication between site supervisors (e.g., primary-grade teachers) and upper-grade teachers who supply the volunteers. This approach allows volunteers to focus on the activity and not be distracted by the need to adjust to strange environments. A disadvantage is that the time spent in the classroom seldom is more than one period because of the demands of the older students' schedule. When a class is missed, students must make up the work. This can be a problem whenever the service is scheduled during the school day unless it is fully integrated into the curriculum. Also, some teachers may be unwilling to permit absences; this is especially the case if they are not well-informed about the objectives.

Community-based   Community-based opportunities for service are virtually limitless, especially in urban areas where settlement houses, hospitals, and community organizations are plentiful. Schine suggests that some activities are more suitable in a non-school base since some youngsters respond more readily to activities sponsored by a community or youth organization. Moreover, some of the practical problems faced by schools in implementing activities do not exist in other settings, e.g., agencies are not constrained by the 50-minute class period or by legislated curricular requirements. Also, a wider range of age groups outside of the school is available where adolescents can assume new roles in fairly familiar environments. Another positive feature is scheduling flexibility. Without the constraints of accommodating to the school calendar, agency-sponsored activities can be planned for varied time periods. Such community-originated initiatives provide greater freedom for students to become involved in community change activities than do school-originated ones. Also, political considerations may place constraints on some kinds of social action in a school-based effort but might be of lesser concern under external sponsorship.

Community-based organizations and schools also can bring complementary resources to the effort. Schine cites the example of a United Way staff member who worked with a school in developing a unit on employment opportunities in the human service field as part of a career exploration curriculum. She concludes, however, that whether an initiative is school-based or community-based, assignments must be real since young people quickly recognize "phony" activities and readily sense and resent exploitation. The service cannot be "busy work," nor should students be assigned tasks that the regular staff wants to avoid.

Shumer's Analysis

Using the "Delphi method" to seek consensus on the characteristics and traits of various initiatives, Shumer (1993) concludes that while consensus exists on some aspects of service-learning, there is still disagreement on several details. Nonetheless, general agreement exists that service-learning can be envisioned through forms or types that are best understood through specific examples. The broad types can be summarized:

School-based initiatives

- Academic classes (required or elective)

- Clearinghouse activities in which students engage in researching and locating service-learning opportunities

- Community service classes

- Co-curricular activities (outside or the classroom)

- District-wide initiatives

- Interdisciplinary projects or courses

- Practica such as apprenticeships, internships, and other forms of field study

- Programs for special populations or "special locations" such as a tutoring project that targets a particular inner-city community or elementary school

- Service hour graduation requirements (e.g., 75 hours in the Atlanta Public Schools and 100 hours in the state of Maryland and in the District of Columbia)

- Statewide initiatives (e.g., Vermont's SerVermont and Pennsylvania's PennServe)

- Vocational education courses including cooperative education and work experience

Community-based initiatives

- Career exploration, e.g., through scouting programs and branches of the military
- "Clearinghouse" efforts (same as above)
- Compensatory services mandated by the court system, e.g., juvenile court-imposed sentences to perform community service
- Conservation Corps
- National service, e.g., the New York City Volunteer Corps where youth assess community needs and design/implement projects to provide needed services
- Programs for special populations
- Service initiatives sponsored by community organizations or institutions
- Short-term projects
- Specific courses or series of courses
- Specific events/crises, e.g., response to natural disasters
- State service programs, e.g., state literacy programs and intergenerational programs
- Summer programs with service components, e.g., Governors' Schools, the Job Training and Partnership Act (JTPA), the National Youth Leadership Council, and the Youth Volunteer Corps
- Vocational programs where private training and skill development are major goals
- Youth community service advisory groups, e.g., Youth United Way and the Points of Light Foundation Initiatives

In short, the types of initiatives can be "sliced" in different ways. But there are many types from which to choose.

• •

How Is Service-Learning
Integrated into the Curriculum?

Examples of Curriculum Integration

Although many educators regard service-learning as a fundamental aspect of curriculum, some observers believe that such efforts often lack purpose and substance and frequently are disconnected from the curriculum (Seigel and Rockwood, 1993). However, the potential impact on the curriculum is apparent. As the Alliance for Service-Learning in Education Reform (1993) asserts, service-learning attempts to make classroom study relevant when students begin to connect their outside service with their work in each curricular area. For example, in SerVermont, approximately 10,000 rural, urban, and suburban K–12 students are involved in their community during the day, after school, and during the summer. The activities include repairing an elderly person's electrical equipment in industrial arts class and typing for nonprofit agencies in business classes (Kendall and Associates, 1990).

Many educators, including Dirks (1993), suggest that in order to be most effective, service-learning must be *integrated* into the curriculum, particularly the civics and government curricula. Its "first home," he asserts, should be subjects that teach citizenship and government, areas which should engage students in community problem solving.

Dirks maintains that students should learn that a "complete citizen" is one who volunteers in a hospital and also understands and votes on bond issues that affect the hospital's future. The students at Hopkins High School in Minnetonka, Minnesota, provide a good example of service-learning as a dimension of a 12th-grade social service class — in this case, "Community Involvement." These students become involved in a variety of community service internships and other activities that are "invented" as they proceed (Kendall and Associates, 1990).

The Association for Supervision and Curriculum Development (1993) also envisions broad integration of activities into the academic curriculum, suggesting, for example, that science students conduct local environmental projects, that art students consider how their art could make life better for others (e.g., donating their art to homeless shelters), and that home economics students use newly acquired skills in cooking and child care to help people in need.

• •

The literature is filled with other illustrations of integration such as Suitland High School's student support/service program in Forestville, Maryland, in which students assist physically disabled adults and other students with learning disabilities. Students at Burbank High School in California work with young children and senior citizens with developmental and physical disabilities, serve as hospital aides, and work at local animal shelters. Students at J.F. Kennedy High School in Plainview, New York, attend classes in which a "Participation in Government" curriculum is utilized. Students at Rainer Beach High School in Seattle are involved in a "Leadership Development" effort as part of school-based management (Kendall and Associates, 1990).

The Council of Chief State School Officers (1994) also provides descriptions of initiatives based on students' age and developmental needs. For example, at the elementary school level, fifth-grade students at the William Penn elementary school in Indianapolis learned of the needs of an elderly school neighbor, Mr. Roberts, who was known for his beautiful garden. These students evidently learned that, because of surgery, their neighbor was unable to do his annual spring planting. With their science teachers' guidance, the students studied planting, pollinating, and growing cycles. In language arts, they read about growing vegetables; in mathematics, they used measurements, multiplication, addition, and division to determine the amounts of seeds and plants needed for a certain area. They also learned how to use tools safely, work together, and encourage each other. More importantly, they got to know Mr. Roberts and to feel pride in their work and the "gifts" they brought to their elderly neighbor's life.

At the Crispus Attucks Middle School, also in Indianapolis, students studied natural disasters as a thematic unit involving social studies, mathematics, science, and language arts. The teachers had heard that the Red Cross needed bandages and supplies and realized that their students might be able to help. The students researched natural disasters, met with Red Cross staff, and discovered that one problem was communication with non-English-speaking people who are involved in disasters. With the help of their Spanish teacher, the students translated a resource booklet for local residents.

At the high school level in Milwaukee, the Northwest Side Community Development Corporation teamed with a predominantly African American high school in order to attract businesses to the community and prepare students with the knowledge, skills, and attitudes to contribute to the work force. The urban rehabilitation Project at Custer High School involved students in a technical education program to rebuild boarded-up houses.

Although these brief examples are only the "tip of the service-learning curriculum iceberg," they bring the classroom into the community and the community into the classroom for part of the students' lives.

Curriculum Integration in Rural Schools

A review of several sources, including Follman, Watkins, and Wilkes (1994) and Kendall and Associates (1990), indicates that the majority of service-learning initiatives appear to be located either in urban or suburban areas where community agencies and organizations are plentiful. Out of approximately 100 examples in these two sources, less than 10 illustrations of service-learning in rural schools and communities were found (excluding those initiatives in SerVermont).

It might appear, then, that service-learning in rural areas is more difficult to implement compared to urban or suburban areas. As Bhaerman (1994) points out, integrating educational, health, and social services in rural areas *is* unmistakably burdened to various degrees by the lack of financial, human, technical, and knowledge resources. However, this is not the case for service-learning in rural schools and communities. Although there can be serious transportation deficiencies and clear limits to the number of volunteers needed by social agencies (a limit quickly reached in many rural areas), a number of "positives" are evident when it comes to service-learning in rural schools and communities.

As rural education consultant Hillman (n.d.) comments, rural citizens have a long history of aiding fellow community members. Rural fire fighters and ambulance medics are volunteers; church suppers often are potlucks in which everyone contributes; and weddings and funerals often are organized with many townspeople working together. Also, when students are involved with service-learning in rural towns, there is a good chance they will be working with a close friend, relative, or, most certainly, a neighbor. Moreover, communication networks already are in place in rural communities since it is possible to gather all the "power brokers" (e.g., the school superintendent, mayor, newspaper editor, Rotary president, and the like) in one room on a regular basis.

Hillman also points to the fact that education in rural areas generally is suffering because of an eroding tax base, low property values, and an aging population that finds it difficult to see the benefit of spending money on education. However, she submits that if older citizens were fed meals made and delivered by high school students and were included in planning a community-wide function, these senior citizens would more likely see schools and students as resources rather than costly drains on their pocketbooks. Hillman, therefore, sees service-learning as "a key to rural regeneration," for she envisions families being more confident that their young people would return from colleges and universities with the desire and skills to regenerate the communities in which they have learned to see themselves as a vital part.

Parsons (1993b) is equally optimistic. As coordinator of the statewide SerVermont initiative, she presents numerous examples of how rural communities have successfully integrated service-learning into the curriculum. Although many of her examples capture the rural tradition of older students helping younger ones, her illustrations are not limited to peer tutoring, landscaping school grounds, and conducting environmental experiments in science classes:

> I know a rural school located a short walking distance from a nursing home. Students regularly "bag lunch" with residents and are allowed to spend free periods at the home. The biology students regularly maintain the home's aquarium, which the industrial arts class built and the biology class originally designed and stocked.
>
> I know another rural school — using community-supplied transportation — that arranges for interested students to "borrow" pets from the local humane society and take them on "visits" to a local nursing home. What they learn during their visits is included in a health class study about mental health. (n. pag.)

Miller (1995) also views service-learning in the context of rural community development. He suggests that by providing rural youth with opportunities to become active, responsible members of a community, they would come to see their communities as a positive choice in which to live, work, and develop rather than leave, abandon, and forget.

The following examples from rural schools undoubtedly are transferable to any school. Clearly, there is great value in looking at service-learning initiatives that are taking place in a variety of settings — rural and urban, small schools and large. Cross-fertilization can occur when we become aware of what is happening in schools and communities unlike our own.

Bremen Public Schools In the "Helping Hands" initiative in Breman, Georgia, service-learning is integrated district-wide in grades K–12. Special education students have designed program activities for pre-schoolers; elementary school classes have "adopted" nursing home residents; middle school students have worked at the nursing home and in Head Start; and in several high school English classes, students dressed as folk heroes, read stories to elementary school students, and visited the senior center to record and publish a book of reminiscences of the elderly (Follman, Watkins, and Wilkes 1994).

Hamilton Middle School At the Hamilton Middle School in Jasper, Florida, seventh-grade students have studied the role, extent, and effects of phosphate strip mining, the major industry in rural Hamilton County. A local chemical company offered assistance, equipment, and two acres of land to the school for a collaborative learning and reclamation project. As a result, students interviewed relatives and neighbors who worked in the mines and reported their restoration plans in the local newspaper and in public meetings. They also have selected native plants and have begun to restore the land, as much as possible, to its natural condition (Follman, Watkins, and Wilkes 1994).

SerVermont   The SerVermont initiative is not confined to rural schools but rather covers the entire state, includes grades one to 12, and involves thousands of students during the school day, after school, and summers. The activities have included tutoring during free periods, repairing elderly persons' electrical equipment in shop courses, and typing for nonprofit groups. Some students are exempted from class to participate, e.g., one school exempts interns for one day during the week and provides make-up materials. SerVermont emphasizes voluntary service and believes that the best service is performed when recipients are involved in planning and when the service is integrated with academics. Community organizations must be involved in developing policies and procedures. Service sites are identified by both teachers and students. The criteria for selecting sites include evident need, opportunities to work with elderly citizens, and activities that deal with environmental concerns (Kendall and Associates 1990).

Rather than a handicap, "ruralness" can be a strength. As Parsons (1993b) concluded:

> Educators know that schools in rural areas have many roles to play for students, and that what we lack in financial resources we need to make up for with imagination and creative resources. One such resource is the integration of help to the community with academic skill building — that is, service learning. (n. pag.)

Although rural schools and communities may be geographically isolated, when they join together in this fashion, they are not isolated in their efforts to transform their educational programs and practices.

. . . .

What Is Service-Learning Instruction?

Out of the Text and into the Context

Service-learning, as one strategy for school improvement, emphasizes academic achievement as a component of the service-learning experience. Service-learning strategies appear to be changing the way some teachers view their classrooms and the ways in which students learn. For example, there appears to be less memorization and "book learning" and more doing and remembering (Briscoe, 1991).

According to Kinsley (1993), the service-learning process evolved by combining the community development theories of Paulo Freire and the educational theories of Ralph Tyler and Hilda Taba — adding a touch of the instructional recommendations of Theodore Sizer, John Goodlad, Jeannie Oakes, and David Berliner — namely, that teachers become "coaches" to their students, involve them in planning their learning experiences, and provide them with opportunities to apply their learning in useful ways.

Service-learning also is rooted in the theories of John Dewey, Jean Piaget, and other constructivist theorists who see learning as the result of interaction with the environment and who recognize that development occurs as individuals strive to construct more satisfying and complex ways of understanding their world. Conrad and Hedin (1989) also restate James Coleman's highly useful contrast of the experiential learning approach with what Coleman calls the more common "information assimilation" model in which the teacher's starting point is presenting information to students followed by one or more steps in this learning sequence:

(1) receiving information,

(2) organizing the information into principles,

(3) inferring a particular application from the general principles, and

(4) applying and revising the principles.

The experiential approach has an alternative sequence in which students

(1) act in a particular situation,

(2) see the effects of that action,

(3) understand those efforts,

(4)   understand the general principles under which the effects fall, and

(5)   apply the principles in new circumstances.

Each approach has strengths and weaknesses. According to Conrad and Hedin (1989), the former approach imparts large amounts of information and systematically develops principles and generalizations. On the other hand, since instruction may "bog down" in the presentation stage and never be applied, little may be learned. In the alternative approach, there is less efficient presentation of information and the danger that students will not draw out principles and generalizations from practice. On the other hand, the experiential approach

> . . . mitigates against the distant abstraction of much classroom instruction and instead places information . . . with the real life nuances and connections which any fact or principle must have to connote genuine and useful meaning; it motivates the learner by providing connections between academic content and the real problems of life; and it aids in retention of knowledge as learning is made personal and applied in action. A sixteen year-old member of an ambulance crew put it more succinctly: "In school you learn chemistry and biology and stuff and then forget it as soon as the test is over. Here you've got to remember because somebody's life depends on it." (19)

Service-learning takes students out of conventional classrooms and introduces them to real tasks, with real consequences, and with substantive learning. Early in this century, progressive educators identified experience as an essential component of meaningful education. They were, in essence, the first modern constructivists who challenged students to find meaning in their actions and to develop their own conclusions.

John Dewey's contribution must be acknowledged, since his conception of education involves several elements that are fundamental to service-learning: experience as a means of obtaining knowledge, active student participation in learning, and community involvement (Shaffer, 1993). First, Dewey saw education as a function of life. Hence, every event an individual experiences becomes a lesson learned; every community in which an individual resides becomes a classroom. Second, Dewey believed that active student participation is central to learning. In fact, he observed that there is no deficit in traditional education greater than its failure to secure the active cooperation of students in constructing the purposes involved in their education. Third, the concept of community is essential in Dewey's pedagogy since in order for students to gain an understanding of the events they experience, they must be able to relate those experiences to situations outside of school. Dewey believed that integrating individuals into society is impossible except when they live in close association with others in the constant free "give and take" of experiences. For Dewey, education is the primary agent of social change within communities. Throughout his life, he maintained that the school should be a genuine form of active community life rather than a separate entity.

Nor should the contribution of Dewey's colleague, William Head Kilpatrick, be overlooked. The modern accounts of service-learning "units" sound very familiar to those of us old enough to remember our first days of teaching along the lines of Kilpatrick's "unit method." Shaffer (1993) does a marvelous job of reconstructing Kilpatrick's work by illustrating a hypothetical service-learning experience (i.e., a clear air campaign) as the focus of a unit of work. He demonstrates that such activities can be used to integrate academic subjects and enhance academic learning. Using the format of a sample unit of the former Lincoln School at Teachers College, Columbia University (where Kilpatrick did much of his seminal work), Shaffer constructs a service-learning "unit" based on the steps of the traditional unit method: instituting a motivational dialogue; identifying problems to be solved and questions to be answered; developing activities in various subject areas that help solve problems; projecting probable outcomes (habits, skills, attitudes, appreciations, and information); and developing new interests leading to further activities.

One of the differences, however, from when Kilpatrick developed his unit methods is that teachers today often begin with content standards, have learner objectives in mind, and have developed tools to assess how well students are meeting the standards. Assessment, indeed, is an essential element in the process since what is tested often is more likely to be taught. The new "CIA," in effect, now stands for the unbroken chain of curriculum/instruction/assessment. Nonetheless, reviewing Kilpatrick's old — in conjunction with Shaffer's new — unit method is like taking a step back in time. Or is it a step "back to the future"?

Perhaps, in time, more teachers will come to accept the view of vonGlasersfeld (1993) and other modern constructivists that knowledge is the result of constructive activities and, hence, cannot be transferred to passive receivers but rather has to be built by each individual. Service-learning provides endless opportunities from which students might construct valuable meanings as they move *out of the text and into the context of real world applications*.

An ancient Chinese proverb says, "Tell me and I will forget; show me and I will remember; involve me and I will understand." Such insights have caused one teacher to conclude that after a dozen years of teaching, it became evident that what worked was students participating actively; what did not work was students sitting passively (MacNichol, 1993). Although this insight may be common knowledge to many teachers, few appear to utilize it in formulating their instructional approaches.

Kielsmeier (1992) similarly concludes that during the past three decades, *what* we have taught has changed significantly; *how* we teach has not. The potential of change, nonetheless, is significant. Kielsmeier contends that the major thrust of service-learning is how it delivers content. Service-learning, he notes, takes *what students should know and should do* and uses it to make schools and communities better places in which to live and work. However, both curriculum *and* instruction need to be enhanced by long-term commitments of schools to professional development programs based on content and performance standards, high expectations, and pedagogical techniques — and not solely on the existence of content standards.

Reflection:
The Key to Service-Learning

One word appears again and again in the writing about service-learning: "reflection." Duckenfield and Swanson (1992) maintain that reflection is the primary component that enables students to think deeply about their experiences because when they think about, write about, and share their thoughts with others, they learn much about themselves and others. Reflection is a skill that involves observing, questioning, and putting new ideas together to add new meanings to the experience. Without it, students are likely to go through the motions but remain unaffected by the experience and left with their personal ignorances and biases reinforced or unexamined (Fertman, 1994).

Other observers agree that reflection is the key to successful service-learning. To the National Society for Experiential Education, critical reflection by the student on what is being learned in the service experience is essential; that service experience alone does not ensure that either significant learning or effective service will occur (Kendall and Associates, 1990). To Kinsley (1993), it is the primary ingredient of success. To the Association for Supervision and Curriculum Development (1993), it is the key for capturing teachable moments. To the Alliance for Service-Learning in Education Reform (1993), it is the process of looking at the implications of actions taken (both good and bad), determining what has been gained, and connecting learning with future actions. Seigel and Rockwood (1993), acknowledging John Dewey, contend that it is not experience alone but rather reflecting upon those experiences that makes a difference in what is learned. Ouellette (1992), a teacher and project coordinator in Duluth, concludes that reflection is essential to learning. His research indicates that students who responded appropriately to his essay questions all posted significant gains in self-concept and problem solving; those who did not participate in structured reflection showed no statistically significant results.

Reflection, however, must be structured and have clear objectives. Activities can be planned yet must be flexible enough to allow learning to occur spontaneously. Duckenfield and Swanson (1992) suggest that reflection must be an interactive, ongoing process and include in-depth discussions, related reading, and journal writing. The Constitutional Rights Foundation (1992c) echoes these ideas, suggesting that systematic reflection should include in-depth questioning and discussion, written and visual activities, and role playing. Reflection, in short, is part of the learning process and not an "add-on." It is, or should be, the key to understanding.

Student Assessment: A Needed Ingredient for Service-Learning

With few exceptions, not a great deal has been written about the impact of service-learning on student outcomes. In fact, McPherson (1991), director of a service-leadership initiative in the state of Washington, believes that the assessment process has been a noticeable weakness of service-learning, noting that although teachers have encouraged written and oral reflection, there has been little systematic examination of this topic. Nonetheless, Ellis (1993), a reading resource teacher in Staten Island, New York, reports that students have developed portfolios that include service-learning activities, evaluated their progress, and discussed ways to improve oral communication skills.

In addition, the Vermont Department of Education (Parsons, 1993a) has launched an initiative to examine how service-learning can be used as a performance-based assessment strategy. This effort includes looking at how service-learning can be used in portfolio assessment and the state's Common Core of Learning. The state education agency has initiated a series of meetings to explore issues related to connecting service-learning to state assessment initiatives. These discussions have included state assessment and testing directors, teachers, service-learning practitioners, and state Learn and Serve coordinators. A continuation and expansion of this initiative is the Department's recently funded National Study Group Network on Service-Learning and Student Assessment. Six state are now involved: California, Colorado, District of Columbia, Minnesota, New Hampshire, and Vermont. Through this initiative, state assessment directors, state service-learning coordinators, and teachers will come together to discuss how service-learning is linked to state assessment requirements, develop sample rubrics and other materials, and share progress in integrating service-learning into district and state assessment programs.

Materials also are being developed in Vermont that include the following exit outcomes: students will participate in a community project, keep a journal that documents performance and personal reflection, write a self-evaluation, and present evaluation and learning results to a community panel. Performance tasks also are being developed, e.g., students will work cooperatively with others, complete a personal action plan that includes individuals' personal responsibility to the group, document activities and reflections, write a self-evaluation, and obtain external validation for the initiative.

To sum up: curriculum, instruction, and assessment must be *unified* if all of these components are to make sense. Cordell (in personal correspondence on June 1, 1995) cogently tied these elements together and, most importantly, coupled them to service-learning when she wrote,

> If service-learning is ever to become a systemic part of curriculum, instruction, and assessment, several factors — besides ongoing support for the process — must be present. The service component must address discipline-based or interdisciplinary content standards established by a state, district, and/or school. These standards should be addressed through learning and assessment events that clearly show how the planning, implementation, and reflection on service demonstrate quality academic learning as well as social responsibility and personal development. Moreover, the criteria for success should be decided by and communicated to the service providers, recipients, and facilitators prior to implementation. The results may be evaluated by each using the established criteria. These examples can then be shared and adapted by others in a similar form. This will help service-learning become part of a repertoire of powerful instructional methods rather than another "fad" imposed on an already cumbersome curricular/instructional agenda.

. . . .

What Are the Major Barriers to Overcome

for Service-Learning to Be Integrated into

Curriculum and Instruction?

Change in education comes slowly. It is not unusual to find teachers exclaiming, "I have taught the traditional way my entire career and so far, so good," or parents stating, "I was taught the traditional way and I turned out OK." Resistance to change, more often than not, is the norm. There are, however, barriers other than the need to overcome locked-in traditions.

Curricular and Instructional Concerns

Schine (1989) observes that one of the most pervasive obstacles to service-learning actually appears under the banner of reform, i.e., a majority of states have legislated requirements that either add more course requirements and hours to the school day or place greater emphasis on standardized test scores. Hence, the reform movement seemingly has resulted in reducing the amount of time for elective and exploratory courses. Schine contends that because of many teachers' concerns about covering a tightly defined curriculum, only a relatively few creative ones find ways to acquire the time needed to plan and implement quality service-learning initiatives.

Other barriers exist when the activities simply become "add-ons." For example, when students miss regularly scheduled classes, they must make up the work, although there seldom are make-up sessions or other available supports. According to Schine, concessions rarely are made in recognizing students' participation, thus making it difficult for those who might benefit the most (i.e., those struggling with academic work who could take advantage of experiential programs). Moreover, relatively few schools — including those at the middle level — use modular scheduling or other mechanisms that permit double class periods or other flexible arrangements. Consequently, it is difficult to schedule service placement, discussion, and reflection. One danger is that service-learning is seen as a frill or a sinecure for the teacher/leader (Schine, 1989).

Schine also acknowledges the debate surrounding "values education." Many teachers find it easier to stick with the "three Rs." The issue raised by Smilow (1993), therefore, is highly relevant, i.e., whether in an already competitively tight schedule students should miss English classes to work in

. . . .

food pantries. Schine likewise notes that a potential problem in relying on community-based sites is that some educators question the willingness of agencies to accept volunteers as young as middle-grade students.

Other observers report that the lack of time is a major barrier. The school day often is overflowing for students who must fit in homework with home duties, meet work obligations, and engage in after-school social activities (Parsons, 1993a). Parsons also raises a related problem — the issue of supervision — since many younger students need extensive supervision and monitoring. Although it has not been discussed widely in the literature, teacher preparation also is a concern. Teachers cannot engage in quality service-learning activities before they have had detailed orientation in planning, implementation, and evaluation. In addition, Parsons (1993b) raises the issue of the relative scarcity and accessibility of quality placement sites, especially in rural areas where little transportation is available to get students to assignments and back to their schools and homes.

Shaffer (1993) sees three unfulfilled needs that could hamper service-learning: the need to define the concept more clearly, to establish explicit outcomes toward which initiatives can strive, and to evaluate the initiatives thoroughly. He argues that the service-learning definition needs standardization so that all efforts have the same characteristics, thus making them identifiable as a distinct instructional approach. He also notes the distinction between service-learning as a way of educating students (academic development) and providing community services independent of the curriculum, whereas others consist of activities that focus on academic outcomes while ignoring community needs. Shaffer, therefore, sees the need for a standard set of criteria so that the concept can be implemented consistently. Although he takes the position that emphasizes learning over service, he believes that no clear understanding of service-learning's true objective exists.

On the issue of outcomes, Shaffer stresses "direct academic" (cognitive) rather than "feel good" (affective) outcomes. Although he concedes that no consensus exists on this issue, he views service-learning as a way of altering the way education is approached and as a means of advancing traditional academic subjects. He also sees the lack of comparable evaluation as a barrier, i.e., the need to measure similar data so that initiatives can be accurately compared. He suggests that evaluations should include standard information about students' academic and emotional development (i.e., grade point averages as well as indicators of self-esteem and self-efficacy) and should emphasize quantitative rather than qualitative data since the latter cannot be easily compared. Such data, he maintains, should include the impact on academic outcomes, dropout rates, test scores, college entrance rates, and grade point averages.

The Council of Chief State School Officers (1995) also has identified a number of relevant curricular and instructional concerns and, indeed, has noted that "much work remains to be done" before service-learning becomes a widely used instructional strategy. The "work" that needs to be done involves the following: time needs to be found for professional development and planning; block scheduling and flexible time frames need to be established; supportive policies and resources need to be in place; and — surely not to be overlooked — skills need to be measured and assessment instruments need to be developed that are not limited solely to pencil-and-paper testing and standardized assessments.

Legal Concerns

A number of legal issues also exist which concern teachers, administrators, and community agency staff. A primary resource organization on legal issues is the Nonprofit Risk Management Center's publication *Legal Issues for Service-Learning Programs* (Seidman and Tremper, 1994). Although we will not explore this issue in depth, we call attention to the many dimensions on which the Center's publication focuses, namely, legal liability fundamentals (e.g., negligence, direct liability for program negligence, liability for harm that volunteers might cause, liability in cooperative programs, and liability shields); injuries to students (including K–12 students, on-campus vs. off-campus activities, harm from intentional misconduct, and workers' compensation); legal limits on service-learning initiatives (e.g., wage/hour, child labor, anti-discrimination laws, and mandatory service); and risk management (controlling risks and insurance).

In order to plan and operate successful initiatives, those responsible for them must be aware of the rules for imposing liability for any harm the initiatives may cause, laws that require or prohibit certain practices, risk management procedures to reduce the likelihood of a negative incident, and insurance arrangements to provide adequate coverage if anything should go wrong. Seidman and Tremper (1994) suggest three points regarding risk control that those in charge should know: what is expected of them, how to perform their duties properly and safely, and when and how to report problems or suggested changes.

. . . .

What Are the Purported Benefits and Results of Service-Learning?

In this section, we review the claims made for service-learning, several evaluation guideposts and challenges, and reported quantitative and qualitative research findings. It is understandable that extensive claims have been made on behalf of service-learning since casual practitioners often become enthusiastic advocates when they believe that they have found a way of teaching that makes sense to them. Hence, they wish to share it with others — and they do — unequivocally.

There are few indications of cost benefits reported in the literature. While there is substantial data in this area about service and conservation corps, that is not the case for the K–12 service-learning. However, Schine (1989), who indicates that service opportunities can be developed without draining a school's financial or human resources, contends that implementation is more efficient when a school can allocate staff and support services. Provisions for transportation, support staff, and a budget for incentives to reward volunteers are desirable. Schine maintains that quality initiatives can be started and sustained at low cost since no extensive supplies or facilities are needed. The indispensable resource is the time teachers need to guide students.

Purported Benefits of Service-Learning

Cairn (1992) categorizes three types of benefits: for students, teachers, and, what he terms, "broader benefits."

Students Cairn (1992) identifies seven benefits for students. They (1) learn to make daily choices about what and how they will learn and, hence, become motivated as they see the relevance of learning and acquire and use new skills; (2) begin to change their traditional role of "receiver" to "producer"; (3) set their own learning goals in relation to the world around them; (4) learn to work in both large and small groups with adults and peers and, thereby, learn to value different perspectives; (5) learn how to respond to social problems, exercise their democratic responsibilities, and gain experiences that help them address social issues; (6) engage in experiences that provide potential material for reflection and action; and (7) demonstrate their mastery of skills and information by using what they have learned to address

. . . .

real needs in real situations. In addition, some teachers report that on days when their students or classes are involved in service-learning activities, attendance is always higher.

Other observers see benefits to students such as increased knowledge about other people and themselves (Kinsley, 1993); character building and positive effects on social, psychological, and intellectual development (Conrad and Hedin, 1989); and enhanced self-esteem, a sense of accomplishment, opportunities for career exploration, and positive attitudes and behaviors relating to the world of work (Schine, 1989). Schine also suggests that service-learning challenges students to work collegially, learn to compromise, learn to communicate effectively, confront problems, consider alternatives, and find solutions to those problems. The consensus appears to be that having "real audiences" for their school work is a powerful motivator for students, since they become more concerned with producing quality products and providing quality services when the results of their work have greater importance than merely pleasing a teacher or earning a grade.

Lastly, the District of Columbia Public Schools (DCPS) — which has a graduation requirement of 100 hours of community service — finds that service-learning promotes its Learner Outcomes which are the characteristics the school system and community value as goals for the students. Although the initiative is not totally service-learning in that experiences are not yet completely integrated into curriculum and instruction, the DC schools are moving in that direction by developing instructional units that incorporate service-learning activities. Cordell (in personal correspondence on June 1, 1995) submitted the following list of DCPS Learner Outcomes.

Students should emerge from the DC Public Schools as:

- *Quality Producers* who effectively communicate information, compute and use technology, and engage in different forms of creative expression.

- *Self-Directed Learners* who exhibit a love for learning, know how to learn, and demonstrate a sense of curiosity and enthusiasm for new experiences.

- *Knowledgeable Problem Solvers* who think independently and consider and apply a broad range of options and strategies in defining and resolving problems.

- *Informed Decision Makers* who anticipate the consequences of their actions and exercise integrity and sound judgment in making consumer and life decisions.

- *Collaborative Leaders* who use effective leadership and group skills to define work and community goals, initiate their accomplishments, enhance personal and others' self-esteem, and sustain cooperative relationships within culturally diverse settings.

- *Community Builders* who are responsible citizens and contribute their time, energies, and talents to improve the health and welfare of themselves and others in their local and global environments.

Many other states and school districts have a set of similar broad characteristics or goals for students which frame academic content standards and reflect community values.

Teachers   Cairn (1992) also presents six benefits for teachers. They (1) learn to guide the instructional process, thereby enlarging their traditional roles of merely transmitting information; (2) become energized by working in new ways with the community; (3) "open up" the schedule by designing activities in which learning can occur on its own schedule rather than "by the bell"; (4) develop theme-based curricula around real-life issues that require both themselves and students to draw on solutions from diverse perspectives; (5) become partners with students, rather than antagonists, as they jointly strive to transform schools into learning communities; and (6) gain active community allies as well as increased resources. Conrad and Hedin (1989) add to this list the notion that service-learning encourages, even forces, academic learning to be tested and applied in the "crucible of real experiences." Lastly, Duckenfield and Swanson (1992) view service-learning as a potentially powerful dropout prevention tool.

Broader benefits   Cairn (1992) identifies two broader benefits of service-learning, namely, that it (1) addresses several factors that research indicates lead to effective learning, e.g., active learner involvement, opportunities for practice, and high but attainable goals; and (2) fuels educational change since it strongly elicits favorable enthusiasm from students, teachers, administrators, parents, and community members. Not only do students and teachers benefit, but so does the community: school and community partnerships are formed to assess, plan, and collaboratively meet identified needs; communities gain a new and important stakeholder, namely, the students; understandings across generations, cultures, perspectives, and abilities are enhanced; and, most importantly, communities acquire valuable services to meet direct human, educational, health, and environmental needs. Last, but certainly far from least, countless benefits are accrued by the recipients of the services. The list is being added to each day as more and more services are provided to both the young and the old.

Reported Results

Hypothesized areas of impact   Conrad and Hedin (1989, 19–20) summarize a range of outcomes that service-learning advocates have developed. The following items, derived from both quantitative and qualitative studies, represent areas of impact rather than operative research hypotheses:

- *Intellectual development and academic learning* — basic academic skills (expressing ideas, reading, calculating); content and skills related to service experiences; higher levels of thinking (open-mindedness, problem solving, critical thinking); insights, judgments, understandings (nuances that cannot be explained in a book or lecture); motivation to learn and retention of knowledge (information); and skills in learning from experiences (observing, asking questions, applying knowledge).

- *Personal growth and development* — ego and moral development; exploration of new roles, identities, and interests; personal efficacy, sense of worth, and competence; revised and reinforced values; self-esteem; taking responsibility and accepting consequences for one's own actions; and willingness to accept new challenges.

- *Social growth and development* — civic participation; career exploration; political efficacy; team work; social responsibility; concern for the welfare of others; and understanding, appreciating, and relating to people from a wide range of backgrounds.

Conrad and Hedin (1989) also caution that service-learning presents unique evaluation problems in that service is not a single, easily defined activity but rather a variety of activities across time and events, each with different potentials for impact. For example, even within the confines of a particular initiative, students might perform different kinds of service; and even if the initiative stresses only one type of service, variations likely will exist in the activities of individual students. Moreover, even if all participants perform the same task, they do not necessarily react or relate to them in the same way.

In short, Conrad and Hedin emphasize that not only is the independent variable — service — difficult to define, but each activity has a wide range of possible outcomes, many of which are hard to assess. A quick perusal of the items above reveals that many of the hypothesized outcomes involve personal characteristics that are very complex, subject to many influences, not likely to be changed in the short run, and not likely to be measured accurately through conventional paper-and-pencil tests. Conrad and Hedin further suggest that many service-learning activities are relatively brief and isolated departures from classroom study, thus preventing evaluators from assessing the cumulative effects of a variety of activities over a period of time. To complicate matters, many studies have been conducted by advocates and/or staff, thereby adding to the potential problem of evaluator bias. The two researchers conclude, however, that while research in this area is difficult, it is not impossible since many sound studies have been conducted that provide useful information, a number of which are described below.

Conrad and Hedin's
Synthesis of Quantitative Findings

Data from several studies show a general trend of social, personal, and academic development fostered by service-learning. Conrad and Hedin (1989) report three types of results: academic learning, social/psychological development, and effects on those served.

With regard to *academic learning,* the strongest results are in the areas of peer tutoring and teaching younger students. For example, in an earlier study, Hedin (1987) reports the results of meta-analyses that consistently found modest increases in reading and mathematics achievements for both the tutor and tutee. Conrad and Hedin speculate that such positive outcomes may be due to the fact that tutoring is the form of service that is most like schooling and the knowledge and skills examined are most like those the tutors have been using. They also cite the findings of Hamilton (1987) that show consistent gains in knowledge when researchers measured information students were likely to encounter in their service experiences.

Two other findings reported by Conrad and Hedin focus on the effects of service experiences on problem solving, open-mindedness, and critical thinking. First, in the mid-1970s, Wilson is reported to have found that students who participated in political and social actions became more open-minded. Second, in the early 1980s, Conrad and Hedin found that students' problem-solving ability — measured by reactions to a series of real-life situations — increased more for students in community service and other experience-based activities than for those in comparison groups; students' ability to analyze problems improved substantially when they encountered problems similar to those presented in the test and where the focus deliberately was on problem solving; and students who had neither discussed their experiences with others nor encountered problems similar to those in the test showed no more change than those in conventional classrooms.

With regard to *social/psychological development*, Conrad and Hedin cite their 1982 study of 27 school-sponsored initiatives that featured direct participation in service activities, career internships, and outdoor adventures in which students showed gains in social and personal responsibility. They also cite a study by Hamilton (1988) of gains in social responsibility with groups of 4-H members engaged in various forms of service. Also, Newman and Rutter (1983) conclude that community service appears to affect students' sense of social responsibility and personal competence more positively than regular classroom instruction.

Conrad and Hedin's 1982 study found that students in service-learning and other experiential initiatives develop favorable attitudes both toward adults and the types of people and organizations with whom they were involved. They also cite Luchs' study (1981) that such students gained more positive attitudes toward others, a greater sense of efficacy, and higher self-esteem than non-participating comparison students; and Calabrese and Schiner's study (1986) that reportedly found lower levels of alienation and isolation and fewer disciplinary problems among adolescents involved in service as part of a program for students with behavioral difficulties.

Self-esteem has been a widely investigated variable. Increases in self-esteem have been reported for students who served as tutors and in more general helping roles. Newmann and Rutter (1983) reported that students involved in community service projects increased on a dimension closely related to self-esteem, i.e., a sense of social competence on such tasks as communicating effectively to groups and persuading adults to take younger persons' views seriously. Mosher (1977) found that moral and ego development can be enhanced particularly by activities that combine discussion of moral issues with the exercise of empathy, role taking, and action on behalf of moral and social goals.

Lastly, with regard to the *effects on those served*, researchers consistently have found tutoring to be an effective mode of instruction, e.g., Hedin (1987) reports that tutoring has been found to be a more effective tool for raising academic outcomes than computer-assisted instruction.

Conrad and Hedin's Synthesis of Qualitative Findings

According to Conrad and Hedin (1989), evidence from qualitative studies suggests even more strongly and consistently that community service is an effective learning method. They assert that persons who have worked with or evaluated service-learning cannot help but be struck by the high regard in which the activities are held by those who are involved with them, including the persons served. It is not unusual for evaluators to observe, as Conrad and Hedin suggest, that even when their pre-/post-tests revealed no significant change, "everyone associated with the [initiative] was highly pleased with it and convinced it was a powerful and positive experience" (25).

Hedin and Conrad (1987) also analyzed journals of high school students who volunteered in schools and social agencies as part of a social studies course. The journals reveal many insights about the new roles they were assuming. For example, one student reports the following feelings about missing one day's assignment:

> As I entered [the school] it was my joy to see Adam wearing a smock covered with paint washing his hands at the sink. "Hi," I said. "Did you go to school yesterday?" he replied shortly. "Yes," I said guiltily (having skipped my service assignment). "Why didn't you come?" he demanded. "I didn't have a ride to get back from here," I explained, thinking as fast as I could. When I started to touch his shoulder, he jerked away and said, "Don't." So I left him alone . . . I felt like a criminal. (26)

Another student reports that service-learning experiences can change the way people look at their lives:

> I cannot even begin to count the number of days that I trudged into [the agency] thinking about all the "huge" problems in my life I was facing: homework, fights with my sister, money for college, the right guy not calling my house, gaining too much weight, missing a party. . . . I cannot think of a single time where I came out not feeling 100% better about life, and also feeling guilty about only thinking negatively about things that are so trivial in my life. (27)

Still another student reveals insights regarding new ways of thinking:

> As the [first] morning came to an end, I began to deeply ponder the reason for my parents telling me to respect my elders. Honestly, I thought, I doubt if I can respect these people [who] wear diapers, drool gallons of saliva a day, [who] speak totally incoherently and [are] totally dependent on a youth. . . . Finally, the first week passed. I became very attached to the residents. I think those insecurities you feel when you start working with elderly people disappear when you begin to really *love* them. (27)

Conrad and Hedin cogently summarize their findings with this concluding thought:

> Through comments such as these, the "more" or "much more" that [these students] said they learned from their service experience began to take on meaning. The "more" turned out to be not so much a reference to amount as to significance, not so much to new information as to more important and more personal knowledge and understanding. The students were probing the fundamental questions of life: Who am I? Where am I going? Is there

any point to it all? They were thinking and writing about the basic issues of adolescence and beyond: about relationship, significance, connection, suffering, meaning, hope, love, and attachment. (28)

[NOTE: Conrad and Hedin's synthesis (1989) also was reported in the June, 1991, issue of Phi Delta Kappan.]

Shaffer's Analysis
of the Impact on Academic Learning

Shaffer (1993) reports data on indirect connections between community service and academic learning in three service-learning efforts — Magic Me, the Community Studies and Service Program (CSP), and Teen Outreach — and concludes that participating students performed better academically in several respects.

With regard to *Magic Me*, a 16-month evaluation of students from two urban and one suburban middle school collected data on self-esteem, locus of control, depression, life satisfaction, attitudes toward the elderly, social support from friends, and youth caring. Data also were collected on attendance rates, suspensions, and grade point averages.

Quantitative findings demonstrated that in all but three affective areas, the participants showed a greater marginal improvement than control students, e.g., on the Rosenberg Self-Esteem Scale, the average scores of volunteers increased by 2.55 points compared to 1.17 points for the control group; on the Meaningful Activity Scale, participants' scores increased an average of 7.44 points compared with 5.48 points for the control group. Shaffer concludes that the initiative is effective in accomplishing its goal of fostering self-esteem by engaging at-risk youth in service with the elderly and the mentally and physically disabled.

Data also suggest that the initiative motivates students to take an active interest in school. Shaffer supports this assertion by comparing attendance and suspension rates for Magic Me and control students. The participants attended school 86 percent of the time compared to 80.1 percent for the control group. Likewise, 35 percent of the control group were suspended during the 1989–90 school year, compared to 8 percent of the service participants. Shaffer believes these modifications contributed to better academic performance for the participants. Although these observations, he asserts, are speculative considering the evaluation was not designed to measure impact of in-school performance, participants received better grades than control students. A comparison of grade point averages shows that the average grade received by participants during the 1989–90 school year was 75.1 percent compared to 72.7 percent for the control group.

With regard to the *Community Studies and Service Program* (CSSP), an evaluation was conducted to assess impact on students' attitudes about the school and community. Data were collected on one's sense of community, self-esteem, self-efficacy, attitudes toward helping others, cultural isolation/awareness, and level of involvement in the school and community. Data also were collected on attendance rates and scores on the California Test of Basic Skills (CTBS). Data indicated that CSSP had a positive effect on all of the affective areas and that students made the greatest progress in self-esteem, self-efficacy, cultural isolation/awareness, and level of involvement in school and community. Data also revealed that participating students attended school more frequently and improved performance on standardized tests compared to non-participating students. Using one school as an example, the average participating student was absent a total of 4.9 days during the spring semester of 1990 compared to the control group average of 8.9 days. Participating students were absent unexcused an average of 3.1 times during the same semester; the control group was absent unexcused an average of 5.9 times. The trend of improved attendance rates for participating students was recorded across all five schools offering CSSP classes.

In order to measure academic progress, the evaluation examined performance on standardized tests. Using a second school as a comparison, substantial differences were recorded on the CTBS Reading, Language Arts, and Mathematics subtests. On each test, participants' scores increased over the course of the 1989–90 school year, whereas scores of the control group decreased, e.g., on the Reading subtest, participating students registered an average score of 46.1 — a net gain of 8.1 points — compared to the control group that had an initial average score of 39.7 and a concluding score of 37.7 — a net decrease of 2 points. Similar data exist for the Language Arts and Mathematics subtests. Shaffer concluded that the primary goal of positively impacting the affective areas is accomplished, and, at the same time, improved academic performance is indirectly achieved. Both quantitative data and qualitative findings in the CSSP in five San Francisco high schools also are reported by Armstrong (1992) who concluded that the CSSP successfully captured the essence of experiential learning as evidenced by the positive feedback from student participants, the students' endorsement of the course, and modest increases in such indicators of academic engagement as grades, attendance, and standardized test performance. In an earlier study, Armstrong and Crowe (1990) reported that the perceived knowledge about community issues increased considerably in a study of approximately 155 students across four schools that participated in the CSSP during the fall of 1989.

Evaluation data on *Teen Outreach* was reported from 1984 to 1989. The initiative had the goal of reducing teenage pregnancy. Hence, the evaluation measured impact on indicators typically associated with high-risk youth:

becoming or causing pregnancy, being arrested, using alcohol or marijuana, and not using contraception when sexually active. Data on suspensions, dropouts, and the percentage of students who failed courses during a school year also were recorded.

Data indicated that Teen Outreach is successful in accomplishing its objective. Between 1984 and 1989, participants consistently had lower pregnancy rates than the control group, e.g., in 1984, 3.5 percent of the participants became pregnant or caused pregnancy compared to a control group among whom 10 percent became pregnant or were responsible for pregnancies. In 1989, 3.2 percent of those participating became pregnant or caused pregnancy, whereas 7 percent of the comparison group became pregnant or were responsible for pregnancies. Similar statistics exist for each year between 1984 and 1989.

In addition, participation positively impacted students' school performance, in that participants were suspended less often, failed fewer courses, and dropped out at a lower rate than students in the control group. During the 1988–89 school year, over 33 percent of the students in the control group were suspended for behavioral problems compared to 14 percent of the Teen Outreach students. Similarly, over 54 percent of the comparison students received an "F" in a course, whereas 39 percent of the students engaged in service activities failed a course. Also, 1.2 percent of the participating students dropped out, whereas 4.5 percent of the control students did not complete the 1988–89 school year. Although the evaluation did not record data on progress in academic course work (i.e., grade point averages), the researcher speculated that students "indirectly" improve academically due to participation in Teen Outreach.

Anderson and Her Colleagues' Study of Two Inner-City Magnet Schools

Anderson, Kinsley, Negroni, and Price (1991) report the development of an "ethic of service" in two inner-city schools in Springfield, Massachusetts: the Lincoln School and the Chestnut Street Middle School. Although most of their report was descriptive, some evaluative data were cited. With regard to the Lincoln School (K–4), participation in community service-learning (CSL) has been a developmental process. Thematic curriculum units have been planned and implemented, e.g., a citizenship theme. Recipients of services include the elderly, patients in children's wards at hospitals, and other students in the school. Anderson and her colleagues report that the school staff now views CSL as a way of increasing student learning, enriching the curriculum, and fostering the spirit of caring and lifetime service. The school staff reportedly engaged in an ongoing process of introspection, analysis, and evaluation to determine how they could deliver educational services to children more effectively. Anderson and her colleagues conclude that students' self-esteem has grown and that this has led to improved academic achievement. Scores on the Massachusetts Test of Basic Skills have increased consistently over three years. The school's climate is reported to be more friendly and students typically are more helpful, kind, and caring.

With regard to the Chestnut Street Middle School, the development of interdisciplinary curricular themes also is central, e.g., "Be a Good Neighbor." Service experiences based on this theme reportedly have given students a sense of local history and an understanding of their relationship to the neighborhood. Although the findings are not specified in detail, the general sense is that a change is evident in the school's climate. Because CSL is not an "add-on," the ethic of service has become pervasive. The integration of CSL into the school's academic life has provided a framework for teaching students to meet their own needs as well as recognize, respond to, and respect the needs of others.

Loesch-Griffin's Findings

Loesch-Griffin and Lobman (1993) evaluated two initiatives: Project Yes (Youth Engaged in Service) in which middle and high school students in the East Bay Area in California mentor and supervise younger students; and the Region 2 Project in which middle and high school students are involved in intensive six-week periods of community service combined with personal growth workshops and a curriculum on environmental conservation and social responsibility. The researchers reported some general data, e.g., 90 to 100 percent of the participants (approximately 80 in a combined follow-up sample) increased confidence in their ability to handle social and academic expectations, and 88 to 97 percent viewed themselves as doing "very well" in their roles as students, including classroom effort and performance and getting along with others.

In a recent expansion of the earlier study, Loesch-Griffin, Petrides, and Pratt (1995) conducted a "final evaluation" of Project YES in which they presented a comprehensive analysis of the skills students reportedly gained through participation in the project. Primarily middle-grade students, a total of 221 who participated in after-school clubs responded to pre- and post-activity questionnaires. Ninety-one were males and 130 were females. The majority of participants were African American (48%) and Asian American (28%); the remaining students were Hispanic (10%), European American (2%), and Native American (1%). The students assessed themselves (when they entered and exited from

Project Yes clubs in which they had participated) on a number of skills. In order of priority, the skills that either developed or increased the most were (1) coming to class on-time, (2) taking risks, (3) completing tasks on projects, (4) enjoying helping others with projects, (5) being dependable for others, (6) feeling comfortable communicating with ethnically diverse groups, (7) taking the initiative to ask questions, and (8) gaining an interest in doing something about community problems. Supplementary observations by the researchers provided additional evidence of the skills and attitudes gained through participation in project activities, particularly in the areas of self-esteem ("a positive activity that they can be proud of") and problem-solving responsibilities.

Kinsley's Findings

Based on an analysis of interviews and a student questionnaire in a case study, also in Springfield, Kinsley (1993) reports the following results when service-learning experiences became part of the learning process: the principal's vision and leadership affected the way the experiences developed; the experiences were used to teach basic skills as well as help students develop social and personal skills; the experiences enhanced teachers' understanding of service-learning as an instructional method; integration of experiences affected how teaching can be viewed as a strategy to enhance educational reform; teachers and students found that the experiences affected their relationships in a positive way; and the experiences gave students an opportunity to develop a sense of community. Kinsley, however, concluded that the implementation process needs to be better understood by both teachers and community partnerships.

Kingsland, Richards, and Coleman's Findings

Kingsland and her colleagues (1995) report the evaluation of the initial year of a comprehensive effort called KIDSNET (Kids Involved Doing Service in New England Towns). The project is a three-year initiative created and managed by the KIDS Consortium, a nonprofit service organization at Southern Maine Technical College in South Portland. A total of 17 schools, 60 teachers, and 1,142 K–12 students were involved during the 1994–95 school year. The principal criteria for project selection were overall and geographic heterogeneity; ethnic and socio-economic composition in the five communities is wide ranging. The sites, representing both rural and urban populations, are Moretown (VT), Lewistin (MT), Norwich (CT), Wells-Ogunquit (ME), and Bath (ME). The four key project goals were (1) to foster a caring and supportive academic climate that will enhance personal and scholastic achievement, (2) to build resiliency and protective factors in youth, (3) to promote a sense of "standardship" for schools and communities among students, and (4) to promote academic achievement among school-aged children and youths. The initial report includes a number of student, teacher, and community "stories" that allowed the researchers to conclude that KIDSNET "appears to be working well" in the five sites in that (1) students, teachers, and community members have given the model strong positive feedback in each of the four goal areas, and (2) high scores in each of the 15 focus group sessions (the research method often used in this study) reflect the fact that people are responding well and believe that the initiative is advantageous to all who are involved. Students are proud of their involvement; teachers believe the projects are suitable for the direction which their various state common core curricula have taken, and community members believe the initiative has helped to foster positive youth/community relationships.

Additional Findings

Duckenfield and Swanson (1992) have reviewed the relationship between service-learning and dropout prevention. While quantitative studies documenting the effectiveness of service-learning in preventing dropouts have not yet been conducted, the researchers feel that a sound base of research on several measurable variables support the claim that service-learning is an effective dropout prevention tool.

Also, Schine (1989) reports that positive results have been gained by 10-to-12-year olds with learning disabilities and behavioral problems in Buffalo, New York. The students, who became tutors for six to eight year olds with similar difficulties, reportedly feel that they are worthwhile themselves and that they, too, can be as productive as anyone.

The literature also includes reports of the positive attitudes of a variety of participants, including Juan Gonzalez, a 1992 graduate of a vocational/technical high school who was motivated through community service; F.W. Wagner, an instructor in refrigeration technology; and Dennis Brunton, a community service-learning facilitation instructor. Gonzalez, Wagner, and Brunton (1993) joined in recording how their experiences changed their lives. In diverse ways, each describes an increase in self-esteem, self-confidence, and self-direction, as well as in-depth knowledge of their community.

Nonetheless, there is an important caveat. Cynthia Parsons (1993a), coordinator of SerVermont, reminds us that it takes considerable time for changes to occur. Although she was discussing service-learning in relation to school dropouts when she observed that it is statistically impossible to improve the dropout rate in a single calendar year, perhaps "a dosage of patience" is needed. Changes will come and reforms will occur if they are thoughtfully conceived and carefully implemented.

. . . .

What Additional

Issues Must Be Addressed?

Accountability

If the kinds of learning and development that service-learning promotes are not among the outcomes by which schools are judged, the approach likely will fare poorly among the various pressures for more standardized curriculum and higher test scores (Conrad and Hedin, 1989). As a response to these pressures, Conrad and Hedin recommend that service-learning goals be clearly articulated and outcomes measured and reported in ways that respond to the accountability demands of the state and local district.

Program Issues

If service-learning were to become part of the school's regular curriculum, Conrad and Hedin (1989) wonder how it might retain its appeal, its "specialness," and its evident departure from the norm. It remains to be seen, they observe, how students would react if service-learning were a routine feature of school life. A related concern is how to make allowances for increased complexity of the activities so that senior high school students are not doing the same things they did at the middle school. A wide array of options will be required that reflect the developmental needs of children and youth. Program developers also must assure that service is an addition to a community's resources rather than a replacement of existing jobs or justification for reducing the public's commitment to promoting social welfare.

Research and Evaluation

Both Kinsley (1993) and Conrad and Hedin (1989) assert that more extensive research and evaluation need to occur in order to establish the credibility of service-learning. Kinsley suggests that procedures such as

. . . .

action research, performance-based assessment, and portfolios are feasible approaches. Conrad and Hedin stress the need for research on what is learned through service, how much is learned, and through what practices these learnings are best attained. This research, they maintain, should involve both quantitative studies focused more precisely on outcomes appropriate to service and qualitative studies that systemically probe the dynamics of service experiences.

Responsibilities and Relationships

Kinsley (1993) sees a need to understand the responsibilities and relationships among school and community partners. If service-learning initiatives are to develop, community partners must understand how they can connect more closely to schools in order to provide extensive service experiences. Based on the teachers' experiences with whom she worked, Kinsley holds that community partners must be involved from the beginning when roles and responsibilities are first defined.

Time and Tradition

Since the typical school day is complete with a "full and tradition-bound curriculum," Conrad and Hedin (1989) question how well service-learning can fit "into a format of groups of 35 students rotating through seven, tightly packed, 47-minute periods" (29). Since such approaches result in there being less direct control over the students' time and movement, practitioners are faced with another burden — unless the school's staff can learn to break away from such time-honored traditions as covering the textbook from the first chapter straight to the concluding index, adhering strictly to pre-ordained lesson plans, keeping the students solidly intact from 8:30 to 3:30, and not diverging from the class discussion under any circumstances.

Professional Development

As Conrad and Hedin (1989) observe, because service-learning is a distinct method that requires new ways of relating to students, training and practice must be available at both the pre-service and in-service levels. They indicate that few pre-service programs are now evident. Moreover, they report that service-learning often works because it is practiced by advocates who believe in it so strongly that they will make it happen in the face of various obstacles. Reluctant and ill-prepared teachers may not feel the same way or share the same success. McPherson (1991) concurs that staff development is essential. Summer institutes in which she has been involved serve to counter this problem. She concluded that when teachers have the opportunity to meet with representatives of community agencies, they develop personal contacts that make future planning easier.

In summer institutes facilitated by NSEE to assist high schools in strengthening and sustaining programs for community service-learning, it was apparent that teachers and program directors needed sessions that dealt with issues related to infusing service-learning into the curriculum as well as sessions designed to share their experiences. Professional development opportunities that allow teachers and program directors the time to explore their work with others in the field can result in rich learning experiences. Because service-learning advocates are often a minority at their school setting, they don't have opportunities to discuss successful strategies or brainstorm solutions to problems they are facing. When given an opportunity to work with other service-learning advocates, teachers can adapt the most successful ideas for their own work. The strength of this type of professional development was demonstrated by the ongoing communication among the participants long after the institutes were concluded.

Voluntary or Required?

A number of school districts and one state have mandated that students perform a specified number of hours in community service prior to graduation. In Maryland, students graduating in 1995 and beyond will be required to perform 75 hours of community service between the sixth grade and the completion of high school in order to receive a diploma (Maryland State Department of Education, n.d.).

A great deal of controversy, however, exists regarding the requirement of service-learning courses and/or hours of service. For example, mandatory service can motivate students who normally might not volunteer; on the other hand, voluntary service attracts students who are truly committed to service and are more manageable since fewer students are involved (Duckenfield and Swanson, 1992). Anderson and her colleagues (1991) believe that making volunteering mandatory is a contradiction in terms and — while it may sound good — is unrealistic. We need to look at both sides of the issue. Additionally, if service-learning is truly a strategy for teaching and learning, it cannot be a mandate for students. Rather, it becomes a mandate for changing the instructional practices of teachers.

Arguments against mandatory service Supple (1992) maintains that mandatory approaches often result in experiences that compromise quality in the interest of meeting performance-hours requirements. Although Conrad and Hedin (1989) acknowledge that numerous examples of schools exist where requiring service appears to have been successful in introducing students to service and meeting community needs, they also acknowledge that the assumption often is made that, if something is good for some, it must be good for all. They observe that mandatory service may well create the image of reluctant teenagers trudging resentfully to — and through — service assignments.

Opponents of mandates also raise these issues: resources may not be available to ensure the necessary training to make service-learning a success if it were mandatory for all students; the opportunity for service credits may have more lasting effect on students who choose to serve than would requiring students to serve in order to graduate; and mandates of any kind often invite political dissension and judicial action (Northwest Regional Education Laboratory, 1994).

The Association of Supervision and Curriculum Development (1993), while acknowledging that experts are divided on this issue, quotes several practitioners who strongly oppose mandatory service:

> "The idea of required service is . . . an oxymoron . . . [it is] very hard to teach anyone what it means to volunteer in a mandatory program. . . . I have yet to find a kid who doesn't think compulsory service has a negative effect. . . ." "Students say a requirement would devalue the fact that they volunteer. . . ." "When unwilling students 'mess up,' not only is that one more failure for them, they are also letting someone else down or even hurting them. It's not like failing geometry . . . this affects others. . . ." "Requiring service undermines the spirit of it [and] tarnishes the young people who are really altruistic . . . by lumping them with all the others." (5)

Other practitioners, the ASCD notes, have mixed feelings:

> "[Although] kids resist what they're forced to do . . . schools make many things mandatory because they're important. . . ." "Students often need a nudge before they become interested in any pursuit, be it geometry, swimming, or community service. . . ." "The real issue [is] the quality of the experience. . . ." "If a school system or state does require service, then it should put the onus on schools to integrate it into the curriculum. . . . It should not be an add-on where students are told they must serve a certain number of hours and then [are] left to find opportunities through service agencies." (5)

Arguments supporting mandatory service   State mandates could relieve financial problems, particularly those associated with transportation costs since state officials may be more likely to supply funding (Portner, 1994). McPherson (Northwest Regional Educational Laboratory, 1994), who remarks that mandates are "not necessarily bad," points to the example of Shorecrest High School in Washington state which requires 60 hours of service linked to the community and the curriculum.

Follman, Watkins, and Wilkes (1994) argue that since the goal of service-learning is to make service an integral part of instruction, the component should not be an "add-on" but rather woven into the "fabric of learning," and that service-learning activities are assignments just as are writing a report or reading a chapter. They suggest that if anything should be mandatory, it should be the opportunity to serve. In fact, they view the issue as "moot," an "unnecessary debate," since when service-learning is integrated into the curriculum, its value for *all* students is self-evident.

The Association for Supervision and Curriculum Development (1993) also quotes several practitioners who strongly support mandatory service:

> "Students who benefit most . . . are the ones who never volunteer. . . . Those who think they're going to hate it end up loving it. . . ." "The experience is so good for so many and life-changing for some. . . ." "Why should we deny any student the joy of serving? We wouldn't deny them the joy of reading. . . ." "Requiring service is a good idea, but only if schools are given time to develop high quality [activities]. . . . Teachers must be prepared to integrate service into the curriculum and students must be oriented." (5)

The Association for Supervision and Curriculum Development strongly supports service-learning. At the 1993 ASCD Annual Conference, a resolution on service-learning was passed:

> As part of their professional and moral responsibility, educators must move boldly to require all students to participate in service learning and other experiences that develop good character and effective citizenship. . . . ASCD urges its affiliates and members to take the lead in establishing required service learning . . . that include all ages, all students and, as appropriate, the curriculum and community. (5)

One of the most thorough analyses of this issue has been presented by Benjamin Barber (1993), Director of the Walt Whitman Center at Rutgers University. Because his insights are exceedingly thoughtful and his message so significant, we have quoted him at some length:

> If the aim of service is the encouragement of voluntarism and a spirit of altruism . . . then clearly it cannot be mandated or required. To speak of coercing voluntarism is to speak in oxymoron and

hardly makes pedagogical sense. But if service is understood as a dimension of citizenship education and civic responsibility in which individuals learn the meaning of social interdependence and become empowered in the democratic arts, then to require service is to do no more in this domain than is done in curricula decisions generally.

To make people serve others may produce desirable behavior, but it does not create responsibility and autonomous individuals. To make people participate in educational curricula that can empower them, however, does create such individuals.

Thinking that the national problem of civic apathy can be cured by encouraging voluntarism is like thinking that illiteracy can be remedied by distributing books on the importance of reading. What young people require in order to volunteer their participation in education-based community service courses are the very skills and understandings that these courses are designed to provide.

There are, of course, problems with mandating education of any kind, but most educators agree that an effective education cannot be left entirely to the discretion of pupils, and schools and universities require a great many things of students — things less important than the skills necessary to preserve America's freedoms. It is the nature of pedagogical authority that it exercises some coercion in the name of liberation. Civic empowerment and the exercise of liberty are simply too important to be treated as extracurricular electives.

This account of education-based service as integral to liberal education in a democracy and, thus, as an appropriate subject for mandatory educational curricula points to a larger issue: the uncoupling of rights and responsibilities in America. . . . The idea of service to country or an obligation to the institutions by which rights and liberty are maintained has fairly vanished.

Civic education rooted in service-learning can be a powerful response to civic scapegoat-ism and the bad habits or representative democracy (deference to authority, blaming deputies for the vices of their electors). When students use experience in the community as a basis for critical reflection in the classroom, and turn classroom reflection into a tool to examine the nature of democratic communities and the role of the citizen in them, there is an opportunity to teach liberty, to uncover the interdependence of self and other, to expose the intimate linkage between rights and responsibilities. Classroom-based community service programs empower students even as they teach them. They bring the lessons of service into the classroom even as they bring the lessons of the classroom out into the community.

[NOTE: The source of Barber's article is the non-copyright monograph edited by Sagawa and Halperin, Visions of Service: The Future of the National and Community Service Act. Washington, DC: National Women's Law Center and American Youth Policy Forum, 1993, pp. 7–8.]

Part II

How Does Service-Learning Link to and Support School Reform Efforts?

What Are the Major Perspectives on

Systemic Educational Reform?

The term, "systemic educational reform," is being heard with increasing frequency in the mid-1990s. Indeed, a rapidly growing knowledge base and a great deal of speculation exist about this concept. There also is no one view of systemic educational reform but rather a variety of perspectives, four of which are briefly described below.

Anderson's Perspective

Anderson (1993) has developed a "continuum of systemic change" which, although presented in a matrix format, does not imply that change is linear, but rather a fluid, dynamic process. She identifies the following six developmental stages and six key elements of change. (See pages 60–61.)

The major components of the sixth and final stage, predominance of a new system, are as follows: the *vision* that all students can learn at higher levels, that learning is achieving and applying knowledge, and that connections are made with other social systems and services. *Public and political support* includes the realization that public, political, and business involvement are essential elements of the process. *Networking* implies that resources are allocated and that networks serve as communication and information channels. *Teaching and learning changes* focus on students who become actively engaged in learning and the use of flexible methods and materials to meet diverse student needs. *Administrative roles and responsibilities* include administrators encouraging innovation and allocating resources to support student learning. *Policymaking and policy alignment* indicate that newly established policies support high student standards, learning outcomes, flexible instruction, and alternative assessment.

Fuhrman and Massell's Perspective

Fuhrman and Massell (1992) observe that support has been growing since the late 1980s for a vision of reform that attempts to pair coordinated state policies with professional discretion at the school site. They view systemic reform as an integration process and organizing principle and indicate that, while the term takes on several meanings, two themes predominate: some educators use the term to refer to comprehensive change in the multi-dimensional aspects of the system, whereas others stress policy integration, coordination, and coherence around a set of clear outcomes. Fuhrman and Massell further suggest that reform strategies encompass policies that influence teaching and learning. In a concluding statement, they cogently summarize the dimensions of systemic reform: unprecedented efforts to integrate diverse policies, new strategies of policy sequencing, novel processes to involve the public and professionals in setting standards, challenges to traditional policies, complex efforts to balance state leadership with flexibility at the school site, extraordinary investment in professional development, and — from our point of view perhaps the most important concept — creative approaches to serving the varied needs of students.

Smith and O'Day's Perspective

Smith and O'Day (1991) propose a design for a systemic state structure that supports school-site efforts to improve instruction based on challenging standards for student learning and policy components tied to the standards that provide guidance about instruction to teachers. Within the structure of coherent state leadership, schools would have the flexibility to develop instructional strategies that are best suited to their students. Emphasizing the need for a common vision of what schools should be like, they also see two sets of values as particularly significant. The first is the collective democratic values that are critical to our society, i.e., "respect for all people, tolerance, equality of opportunity, respect for the individual, participation in the democratic functions of the society, and service to the society" (246). The second set relates to the attitudes and tasks of teachers and students, i.e., "to prize exploration and production of knowledge, rigor in thinking, and sustained intellectual effort" (246). They maintain that these values exist in latent form in most citizens — especially teachers — but need "to be awakened" in order to permeate the system. Moreover, they suggest that "these values can help nourish and sustain over time environments in the school that can intellectually stimulate and engage ALL children in the way that we should expect" (26).

O'Day and Smith (1993) elaborate on the basic characteristics of an idealized version of a model of systemic reform, including curriculum frameworks that establish what students should know and be able to do, and alignment of state policies that provide a coherent structure to support schools in designing effective strategies for teaching the content of the frameworks to all students. Through a restructured governance system, schools would have

The Continuum of Systemic Change

	Stages of Change		
Elements of Change	**Maintenance of Old System**	**Awareness**	**Exploration**
Vision	Vision reflects: ♦ Learning based on seat time ♦ Teaching as lecture ♦ Mandates and inputs ♦ Education system separate from social service systems	♦ Multiple stakeholders realize need to change ♦ Strategic plans call for fundamental changes	♦ Stakeholder groups promote new ideas for parts of system ♦ New examples debated ♦ Growing numbers and types of stakeholders drawn together
Public and Political Support	♦ Support taken for granted ♦ Only a concern when finances are needed ♦ Public informed, not engaged	♦ Policymakers, media discuss need for changes ♦ Public forums on change	♦ Task forces formed ♦ Leaders speak on some issues ♦ Minor resource allocation ♦ Public involved in redefining learning outcomes
Network-ing	♦ Networking seen as insignificant ♦ Partnerships are one-shot, supplemental	♦ Networking valued ♦ A critical mass of teachers explore joining networks ♦ Realization that partnerships need to be longer-term, integral	♦ Networks (including electronic) share information ♦ Schools, districts, and states join networks ♦ School leaders contact potential partners
Teaching and Learning Changes	Emphasis on: ♦ Standard curriculum ♦ Delivery of Information ♦ Standardized tests ♦ Raising scores	♦ Recognition that current research is not used in teaching, and that education problems are due to broad social, economic, techno-logical changes	♦ Resources committed to learning new teaching methods; multiyear commitments ♦ New modes of assessment explored ♦ Outcomes are defined
Adminis-trative Roles and Responsi-bilities	Responsibilities seen as: ♦ Diminishing conflict ♦ Emphasizing standardiza-tion, rules ♦ Providing information ♦ Top-down decision making	♦ Administrators recognize need to change roles ♦ New roles, responsibilities discussed ♦ Media attention on innovative leaders	♦ Site-based decision making piloted ♦ Professional development focuses on new roles ♦ Bureaucracy questioned ♦ Some resources allocated to learning outcomes
Policy Alignment	Policy emphasizes: ♦ Textbook selection ♦ Standardized teaching, tests ♦ Comparisons among schools on student achievement ♦ Hierarchical structure	♦ Experimentation promoted ♦ Recognition that standard-ized tests don't measure all learning outcomes; low achievement may be due to conditions beyond teaching	♦ New assessments explored ♦ Policies defining gradua-tion based on demonstrated learning piloted ♦ Curriculums emphasize higher learning for all

Note: Users may add features to the matrix cells to better depict their situation. Not all features of every stage have been included.

...ansition	Emergence of New Infrastructure	Predominance of New System
...merging consensus ...ld components shed ...eed for linkages understood	♦ Vision includes student outcomes, system structure, underlying beliefs ♦ Continual refinement of vision, expanded involvement	♦ Belief that all students can learn at higher levels ♦ Learning is achieving and applying knowledge ♦ Education connected to social services
...ublic debate ...eaders campaign for change ...esistant groups vocal ...ore resources allocated ...iversity recognized	♦ Ongoing task forces ♦ Resources are ongoing; emphasis on meeting diverse student needs ♦ Public engaged in change	♦ Public, political, business involvement essential ♦ Allocation of resources based on new vision
...etworks recognized as long-...m features ...ebates on how to support ...oing networks ...isenfranchised groups use ...works for empowerment	♦ Networks accepted practice; major source of new knowledge ♦ Empowerment issues debated ♦ Multiple partners support vision	♦ Resources allocated for networks ♦ Networks serve as major communication channels ♦ Power is shared
...eachers, schools, districts try ...v approaches ...eachers given time to plan ...ecognition of change needed ...l resources required ...hanges assessed	♦ Assessments encourage improvement, recognize uneven progress ♦ Graduation based on outcomes ♦ Teaching engages students ♦ Ongoing teacher development	In most schools: ♦ Student learning is active ♦ Assessments are focused on outcomes ♦ Teacher and administrator preparation uses outcomes
...ethods developed to distribute ...cision making ...mphasis on outcomes to be ...ieved; flexibility in how ...esources for ongoing teacher ...fessional development	♦ Administrators hired using new criteria ♦ Site-based decision making ♦ School-community councils ♦ Teachers responsible for instructional decisions	Administrators: ♦ Encourage rethinking, improve-ment, innovation ♦ Allocate resources to support student learning ♦ Use site-based management
...ask forces define learning ...comes ...chools have latitude to ...esign teaching and learning ...ecognition that policies need ...iew	♦ Exit outcomes developed, emphasize complex learning ♦ Multiple means of assessment ♦ Major review of policy ♦ Education and social service policies connected	Policy supports: ♦ Ongoing improvement ♦ High student standards ♦ Learning outcomes ♦ Flexible instruction ♦ Alternative assessment

Anderson, B. (September 1993). "The Role of Service Learning and Educational Reform." *Educational Leadership*, 51, 1: 14–17. (Matrix, pages 16–17.)

· ·

the resources, flexibility, and responsibility to design and implement effective strategies for preparing students to learn the content of the frameworks to a high level of performance. O'Day and Smith also expand their views on equity and access by re-emphasizing that the tenet that *all* children should have access to challenging content is at the heart of content-based reform. They base this on two assumptions: that deep understanding of academic content, complex thinking, and problem solving are not only desirable but are necessary for responsible citizenship; and that *all* children can acquire these skills.

Sashkin and Egermeier's Perspective

Sashkin and Egermeier (1993) present four "operational strategies" — change models and processes — for improving school performance, namely, fixing the parts, the people, the school, and the system.

The notion of *fixing the parts* — curriculum, instruction, and assessment — has several dimensions: transferring and implementing innovations; providing technical assistance to schools so that dissemination and adoption become a problem-solving process rather than simply adoption of innovations; and providing "high-quality information . . . and small amounts of funds to local schools [that] can be effective in promoting improvements in schools" (5).

The notion of *fixing the people* also has several dimensions: developing strategies for professional and institutional reform based on changing the school's culture; improving the knowledge and skills of teachers and administrators and helping them to better perform their roles; improving both pre-service and in-service education; and incorporating three approaches (initially identified by Fullen), i.e., adopting innovations, using staff development as an innovation in its own right, and linking classroom improvement to school improvement.

Fixing the schools involves developing organizational capacity for solving problems and making improvements; identifying problems, diagnosing their causes, and determining whether and how well the actions designed to solve problems actually work; and changing the culture of an organization so that it is better able to adapt and solve problems.

The most current change model, *fixing the system*, includes

(1) reforming the entire enterprise — from national goals, to state curriculum frameworks, to district curriculum, and to classroom teaching and learning;

(2)   incorporating the previous three strategies (fix the parts, the people, the school) into a broader context that extends to the national level, state education agencies, professional development institutions, communities, and school districts;

(3)   incorporating various elements of restructuring, including decentralizing authority (site-based management); providing authority consistent with responsibility (accountability); changing governance patterns (empowering parents and community members); and uniting parents, educators, businesses, universities, foundations, and the public into a collaborative force in order to transform relationships between schools and communities; and

(4)   developing more integrated and cohesive curricula, state curriculum frameworks, achievement and performance standards in all curricular areas, and improving instruction by developing more authentic ways of ascertaining what students know and can do.

. . . .

What Are the Service-Learning Connections to Federal School Improvement Initiatives?

S tates and school districts are currently engaged in various stages of planning for and/or implementing three pieces of national legislation that have major implications for promoting service-learning: the Goals 2000: Educate America Act, the Improving America's Schools Act , and the School-to-Work Opportunities Act. Each of these have the potential to forge stronger connections between service-learning and school improvement efforts nationally.

Goals 2000: Educate America Act

This legislation calls for the development of comprehensive state education strategies that result in the attainment of the national education goals and lifelong learning systems. Under Goals 2000, categorical programs that address specific phases in youth education and development must now be viewed as part of a system with many reinforcing and essential elements. Under Goals 2000, diverse programs dealing with early childhood, elementary, middle, and secondary education, as well as education for employment preparation, must begin to function as part of a coordinated continuum of positive development and preparation for life. GOALS 2000 includes codifying the National Education Goals, encouraging the development and use of high academic standards for all, creating an incentive grant program for states to support comprehensive reforms, providing funds to states for teacher training and professional development, promoting parent and community involvement, and promoting "bottom-up" education reform in every school and community.

Service-learning is a "bottom-up" strategy that can help states and schools achieve the eight National Education Goals and promote meaningful community involvement in the educational process of all students.

Improving America's Schools Act

This Act is the primary federal source of support for public schools, particularly those that serve disadvantaged children. The focus is on upgrading instruction, professional development, and accountability, and

. . . .

aligning these elements with high standards. Many provisions of this Act are geared to enabling children and youth to meet challenging content and student performance standards — dimensions of systemic educational reform.

The Council of Chief State School Officers (n.d.) notes that service-learning and related strategies are included in the various program areas of this Act as an allowable use of funds. The following is a brief overview of several provisions most directly related to service-learning:

Title I — Under schoolwide programs and professional development activities, service-learning and applied learning are included as effective strategies for improving learning, instruction, and curriculum for helping disadvantaged children meet high standards.

Title II: Dwight D. Eisenhower Professional Development Program — Funds are provided to assist states, local educational agencies, and institutions of higher education with teacher education programs. Funds may be used to train teachers in such interactive teaching strategies as service-learning, experiential learning, career-related education, and environmental education that integrate real work applications into core academic subjects.

Title IV: Safe and Drug-Free Schools and Communities — Funds support programs to meet the seventh National Education Goal by preventing violence in and around schools and by strengthening programs that prevent the illegal abuse of alcohol, tobacco, and drugs, and involve parents. Programs are coordinated with related federal, state, and community resources through the provision of federal assistance to states and local educational agencies; to states for grants to and contracts with community-based organizations to conduct training, demonstrations, and evaluations; and to institutions of higher education to establish, operate, expand, and improve programs of school drug and violence prevention. States and local schools and communities may use funds for developing and implementing community-based drug and violence prevention programs that link community resources with schools and integrate services involving education, vocational and job skills training and placement, law enforcement, health, mental health, community service, mentoring, and other appropriate services, and for developing service-learning projects that encourage drug- and violence-free lifestyles.

Title X: Programs of National Significance — Service-learning is listed under Fund for the Improvement of Education, a program to support nationally significant programs to improve the quality of education and help all students to meet the challenging state content standards and achieve the National Education Goals. The Secretary is authorized to make grants or contracts with state and local education agencies, institutions of higher education, and other public and private agencies, organizations, and institutions; agreements with gifted and talented children's programs to assist state and local education agencies, institutions of higher education, and other public and private agencies and organizations to initiate and coordinate programs of research, demonstration, and personnel training designed to build capacity in elementary and secondary schools to meet the special educational needs of gifted and talented students; and Urban and Rural Education Assistance grants to eligible local educational agencies serving an urban/rural area or state educational agencies designed to assist in local school improvement and reform efforts.

Also, it is important to note that schools and communities have been using funds from these programs under the Elementary and Secondary Education Act for service-learning for some time as a means of improving teaching and learning. The changes in the new law merely incorporate the term "service-learning" in the programs listed above.

School-to-Work Opportunities Act

This legislation establishes a national framework within which all states can create high-quality, statewide school-to-work opportunity systems designed to help youth identify and select paths to productive and progressively more rewarding employment. The Act requires that these systems be part of comprehensive efforts for education reform and be coordinated with recent reforms in vocational education and other national initiatives.

The Council of Chief State School Officers (1996) points out a number of commonalties between service-learning and school-to-work (or school-to-career) initiatives in that both are forms of experiential education that extend student learning into the community and worksite, both provide students with contextualized learning opportunities, and both help develop organization and problem-solving skills as well as the competencies and skills that are important for employability and responsible citizenship. Service-learning, the CCSSO continues, is one of the major strategies that help students transition from school to employment. CCSSO also views service-learning and school-to-work "on a continuum of learning within a context of educational reform" that would, among other things, provide opportunities for students at all levels to explore a wide variety of careers and prepare them to make more informed employment and college decisions. "This type of coordination between these national initiatives," the CCSSO concludes, "is how systemic education reform will become a reality in schools across the country and benefit all students and communities" (4).

The Council of Chief State School Officers (1995) includes service-learning in its policy reference document for states as one of the strategies to help students transition from school to employment. For children, service-learning offers exposure to the world of work and community and provides a context for building academic and work-readiness skills. For youth, it offers valuable exploration into and experience with real-world needs that can be addressed through action and initiative, while further solidifying their work-readiness, academic, and technical skills. Service-learning represents a holistic approach to youth development and the building of multiple competencies. It is not limited to unpaid experiences or internships in nonprofit or public sectors; many programs offer stipends or other benefits and can be found in numerous sectors.

A number of prominent school-to-work observers see a close connection with service-learning. For example, Kenneth Hoyt (1994), the primary advocate of career education for the past 25 years, recognizes "the reality and importance" of both paid and unpaid work in school-to-work transition (although he prefers the term "school-to-employment"). Mendel (1994) similarly views service-learning as a possible alternative to youth apprenticeships since a significant number of employees may be unable to participate in a youth apprenticeship system. He suggests that schools might wish to concentrate on apprentice-like or simulated workplace activities as well as service-learning. Hamilton and Hamilton (1994) assert that all young people should engage in community service since it gives them experiences similar to work even though the experiences are unpaid. Since such unpaid experiences may lead to paid work experiences of some young people, those experiences could be the only form of work-based learning for some students. The relationship between the two approaches is illustrated in what the Hamiltons have termed "learning opportunities at school and work."

....

How Are States and School Districts Relating Service-Learning to School Reform?

A number of states have begun to design service-learning initiatives that take a systemic approach to infusing the concept into the broader view of educational reform and youth development (Council of Chief State School Officers, 1993). In most cases service-learning is a recommended strategy for achieving the goals of state school improvement efforts in areas of content standards, instruction, and/or assessment. The following are examples of some state initiatives.

California has developed service-learning standards that outline what students should know and be able to do as a result of their participation in a service-learning activity or project. The intent of these standards is to assist local school districts in incorporating service-learning into curricula across the content areas as a way of achieving state and school district curriculum standards.

The **Colorado** Department of Education is integrating service-learning into its New Standards Project by developing a "how-to" manual for connecting service-learning with performance-based assessment strategies that encompass reading, writing, mathematics, science, history, and the social sciences.

The **District of Columbia** is expanding its 1992 school board mandate that requires students to complete 100 hours of community service for graduation. A new school system policy promotes service-learning and connects it to content standards and framework documents. One goal of this new policy is to engage all teachers in the use of service-learning as an educational strategy in implementing performance-based education. Another goal is to use service-learning as one avenue in its school-to-career pathways plan. Service-learning is mentioned both in the curriculum framework documents and in the Goals 2000 plan.

Delaware is connecting service-learning to the state's multi-year school reform effort, "New Directions for Education," initiated by the Delaware Board of Education in 1992. One of the most important objectives of "New Directions" is to teach students through active participation in learning events that have meaningful application and clear purpose. One way in which the state's school-based initiative is attempting to link service-learning to the broader reform is by developing performance-based assessment tasks and learning/

assessment units through which students acquire and demonstrate knowledge in conjunction with instructional activities based on the state's content standards.

In **Kentucky**, service-learning is promoted as an effective strategy for achieving the learning goals outlined in the state's education reform act. The student learning goals include: apply core concepts and principles from mathematics, the sciences, the arts, the humanities, social studies, and practical living studies to situations students will encounter throughout their lives; become responsible members of a family, work group, or community, including demonstrating effectiveness in community service; and think and solve problems in school situations and in a variety of situations students will encounter in life.

Minnesota is linking its service-learning initiatives to the state's school-to-work initiatives. Recently the state board voted to make service-learning a strategy for achieving the curriculum standards in all content areas.

Oregon included service-learning as a innovative educational strategy in its Goals 2000 plan and has encouraged school districts to include service-learning in school-to-work implementation plans.

In **South Carolina**, service-learning has become an integral part of the state department of education's push for Total Quality Education. The state views service-learning as being an integral component for producing fundamental reform throughout the state.

Vermont has linked its service-learning initiatives to current education reform efforts such as the state's Common Core of Learnings, Goals 2000, and school-to-work transition. It has also requested that school districts engage in a state-led pilot portfolio assessment project using service-learning as a primary strategy.

This handful of state examples represents the current move in most states to integrate service-learning into educational reform activities at the state and local level. Whether the connections are to improvements in instruction, curriculum, or assessment, it is clear that states consider service-learning a potentially effective method to help students achieve high standards of learning.

. . . .

How Do Educators View Service-Learning and School Reform?

S ervice-learning has been described as both the "sleeping giant" and "Trojan horse" of school reform. Nathan and Kielsmeier (1991) acknowledge that while no single strategy will transform every student or regenerate every school, integrating service and social action into academic programs will aid students in thinking more analytically and enhancing higher-order skills — two key goals that often appear in the reform literature. Hence, they portray service-learning as a "sleeping giant" in the reform movement, a force that can produce changes not imposed from above but rather that build on local circumstances.

McPherson sees service-learning as a "Trojan horse," i.e., although the concept at first glance looks simple, "it actually becomes much more than what people had originally thought" (Northwest Regional Educational Laboratory, 1994, 5). Indeed, it has great potential for creating an environment for restructuring the school day and for challenging the community to view itself as a "co-educator" with the school.

Although no other observers use such graphic metaphors, some educators view service-learning as a major component of educational reform along with curriculum/instruction, school organization, technology, and monetary incentives. Supple (1992) suggests that service-learning can significantly transform relationships between schools and communities. Jones and Gentry (1993) see the approach as a vehicle for school reform and improvement by incorporating activities into instruction in a context of open discussions centering on persistent democratic concerns.

As noted previously, the Council of Chief State School Officers (1994) sees service-learning as a component of educational reform in that service-learning is a *pedagogy* that incorporates high standards and performance assessments into the school's agenda, involves students as persons responsible for their own learning, and utilizes teachers as coaches; a *philosophy* that encourages a community of learners who collaborate to improve a school's culture and governance; and a *process* that facilitates school/family/community partnerships.

Sagawa (1993), describing a U.S. Senate debate on the National and Community Service Act, reports that reforming the education system through service-learning was one of the reasons many Senators favored the legislation. Perrone (1993), who sees service-learning as a means of revitalizing schools, also argues that the approach needs to be more than a one-shot activity. Clark (1993) suggests that service-learning must be linked with the curriculum as part of the reform agenda. Schine (1989) advocates that

. . . .

service-learning must be viewed as part of middle school reform. Unfortunately, the "Trojan horse" and "sleeping giant" analogies might imply to some that service-learning is a strategy that has to slip in the back door or that teachers have to be "sneaky" about infusing it into the culture of a school.

Earlier, we noted that Conrad and Hedin (1989) distinguish between *youth reform* and *educational reform*. The heart of the youth reformer's case is that there is a massive need to engage youth in meeting the demands of democracy, whereas the focus on educational reform centers on "the power of service to meet the basic objectives of schools: promoting the personal, social, and intellectual development of young people and preparing involved and effective citizens" (18). The authors of this paper believe that the two reform efforts are inseparable, since the object of both are the children and youth who attend our schools. One cannot reform "the system" simply for reform sake alone; students are the bottom line.

Practitioners who have written about their experiences in transforming the school's culture offer a wealth of insights. One such person, Roland MacNichol (1993), a teacher at Gig Harbor (Washington) High School, has reflected on his experiences. Because his insights are so valuable, we cite them at some length:

> For me the idea of a school culture is important when we think about the kind of school community we work in and what kind of human beings our students are when they leave us. Service-learning can have a profound effect on a school's culture because it changes both belief systems about how education works and what we do in the classroom.

> Changing the culture of a school community is no small task. It takes a serious commitment on all levels. Without knowledge of a school's culture, it is impossible to change. This makes a strong argument for site-based decision making. We have all observed top-down mandates for change go the way of bell-bottom jeans. Every building has some people who immediately see the tremendous potential of service-learning. It is imperative to train, support, and celebrate their successes.

> In order to facilitate change, it is easiest if one finds a variety of ways to infuse service into all parts of the school's culture. Initially, honoring the existing traditions and culture of the school and building on these traditions legitimizes and roots service-learning in the school culture. (10)

He further explains that

> As we begin to transform the culture of our school community, we can move forward by celebrating what we already do in our

school. Many schools have long supported food and clothing drives, recycling, and many forms of cooperative learning. All of these activities are forms of service. By deliberately using the term "service" when we speak of helping each other in even the simplest kindness, we begin to change our school community. Language plays a powerful role in shaping our beliefs and behaviors. I have seen peer editing used in many elementary, middle school, and high school classes as students learn the writing process. If we introduce peer editing in our schools as "service," it changes the context of the process and the classroom.

Or schools can become cultures which recognize service as important and celebrate service on many different levels. The idea that the school community values every kind of service is essential to truly changing a school's climate. No kind of service is any more or less valid, and service can occur at many different levels: service to each other, to family, to school, to community, or to the environment. Service can be a one-time kindness or an ongoing commitment. They all make a difference and they all speak loudly about what our school community is all about and who we are. (11)

MacNichol concludes that

Ultimately, this change in the culture of our schools creates a need to examine the structure, schedule, and curriculum so that institutional structures support active service-learning. It also encourages us to create service experiences that are meaningful to young people, that meet genuine needs, and that nurture deliberate and rich learning. Service-learning is the right thing to do in helping make our schools thoughtful, caring places with strong belief systems based on service and on young people making a difference.

The challenge is not easy. Service-learning is not a task to accomplish, but a path to take to find better ways to educate and teach young people. At our school, we have found as we move slowly down this path we have to compromise our ideals less; there is more meaning in what we do; we honor young people more; and we find more hope that this world can be a better place. (11)

[NOTE: Reprinted with permission of Greenwood Publishing Group, Inc., Westport, CT, Copyright 1993. Also, for additional suggestions about transforming a school's culture to include service-learning, see Appendix A (Principles, Standards, Steps Along The Way, and Guideposts). Curriculum guides and several service-learning organizations that can provide additional suggestions are included in Appendices B, C, D, and E.]

Although MacNichol is only one teacher and Gig Harbor is only one high school, together they show a way that the school's culture can be positively altered, particularly when community services are aligned with the students' academic, social, and personal development.

. . . .

How Does Service-Learning Converge
with Systemic Educational Reform?

In this concluding section, we summarize the major components of the two strategies and illustrate the areas in which they converge.

Systemic Educational Reform:
Predominance of a New System

At the outset, we stated that in her "continuum of systemic change," Anderson (1993) called the sixth and final developmental stage the *predominance of a new system*. Using Anderson's categories, we have summarized what she, Fuhrman and Massell (1992), Smith and O'Day (1991), and Sashkin and Egermeier (1993) have identified as the key elements of a reformed educational system.

Visions of a new educational system The most fundamental vision is that all students can learn at high levels, that learning is constructing meaning and applying knowledge, and that connections are made with other social systems (Anderson, 1993). Activities are based on the democratic values of respect for all people, tolerance, equality of opportunity, participation in the democratic functions of society, and service to society (Smith and O'Day, 1991).

Public and political support Public, political, and business involvement is an essential element of educational reform (Anderson, 1993). Processes are developed to involve the public and the profession in setting educational standards (Fuhrman and Massell, 1992).

Networking with partners Networks serve as vital communication and information channels (Anderson, 1993). Parents, educators, businesses, universities, foundations, and the public unite in order to transform school/community relationships (Sashkin and Egermeier, 1993).

Teaching and learning changes Students are actively engaged in learning; flexible methods and materials are used to meet student needs (Anderson, 1993). Creative instructional approaches are developed to serve the varied needs of students (Fuhrman and Massell, 1992). Extraordinary

. . . .

investments are made for the professional development of school personnel. Also, school site efforts are planned to improve instruction; the process is based on challenging standards for learning; attitudes and tasks of teachers and learners prize the exploration and production of knowledge, rigor in thinking, and sustained intellectual efforts; and curriculum framework documents establish what students should know and be able to do (Smith and O'Day, 1991). School systems and schools are concerned with integrating all of the critical parts — curriculum, instruction, and assessment; professional and institutional reform strategies focus on changing the school's culture; integrated curriculum is developed in all subject areas; and instruction is improved by developing authentic ways of ascertaining what students know and can do (Sashkin and Egermeier, 1993).

Administrative roles and responsibilities   Administrators encourage rethinking and innovation and allocate resources to support student learning (Anderson, 1993). Through a restructured governance system, schools provide the resources and flexibility to design and implement effective strategies for preparing students to learn the content of the curriculum frameworks to a high level of performance (Smith and O'Day, 1991). Decentralized authority (site-based management) and authority consistent with responsibility (accountability and shared decision making) are central features of the process (Sashkin and Egermeier, 1993).

Policymaking and policy alignment   Policies support high student standards, learning outcomes, alternative assessment, and flexible instruction (Anderson, 1993). Unprecedented efforts exist to integrate policies; new strategies exist for policy sequencing; challenges to traditional policies are made and efforts are made to balance state leadership with flexibility at the school district and school site (Fuhrman and Massell, 1992). Policy components are tied to standards and reinforce one another in providing guidance about instruction to teachers (Smith and O'Day, 1991). Alignment of state educational policies provide a coherent structure to support schools in designing effective strategies for teaching the content of the frameworks to all students (Sashkin and Egermeier, 1993).

These changes, it should be noted, in many cases represent the idea rather than the current reality. The current reality is the fact that, more often than not, most school districts are constrained by fewer and fewer resources. Nonetheless, these are important criteria with which to assess the development of a new system.

Service-Learning:
Potential for a New System

Service-learning holds a great deal of potential for contributing to this emerging new system. The concept is highly consistent with the elements of systemic educational reform, particularly the common focus on transforming relationships between schools and communities; linking curriculum/instruction/assessment; developing integrated, cohesive curricula; and improving instruction by having students demonstrate what they know and, through application, what they can do.

Visions of a new educational system   As stated earlier, President Clinton envisions schools where young people are involved in community service in a variety of ways. Many educators share his vision. Service-learning, indeed, is a powerful tool through which academic and social objectives of education can be accomplished and through which teaching and learning can advance the ethic of civic responsibility by developing caring and compassionate citizens and through relevant applications with "real" purposes and audiences (Shaffer, 1993). The approach is intended both to invigorate education and to mobilize youth as partners in the process (Senate Bill 626, 1993). Most importantly, service-learning is viewed as a philosophy that encourages the creation of a caring community of learners who strive to improve the school's culture and governance (Council of Chief State School Officers).

Public and political support   One of the fundamental principles of service-learning is that it must have ongoing commitment and support from all of the involved stakeholders (Honnet and Paulsen, 1989). One of its basic standards is that the approach be understood and supported as an integral element in the life of a school and its community (Alliance for Service-Learning in Education Reform). Service-learning is becoming recognized for its contribution to both schools and communities and, as a result, is being initiated and/or enhanced in a number of school districts throughout the country.

Networking with partners   One major aspect of service-learning is identifying and addressing community needs at the same time student needs are being met. This reciprocity, indeed, is a major difference between service-learning and simple volunteerism. Moreover, in order to be successful, service-learning experiences must be developed in collaboration with communities (National and Community Service Act of 1990). The community is intrinsically involved in the educational process (Shaffer, 1993). Conversely, service-learning is a process that facilitates a community-wide strategy to improve both the quality of education and the quality of life in a community (Council of Chief State School Officers). The concept of networking with partners is a central feature in service-learning, as it is in systemic educational reform.

Teaching and learning changes   It is in the area of teaching and learning — curriculum, instruction, and assessment — where service-learning and systemic educational reform most directly converge. Service-learning can be an organizing principle for the total academic program since, when it is infused into the K–12 curriculum, the school becomes structured to serve the community and, at the same time, reach all students (Duckenfield and Swanson, 1992). The entire community becomes a resource for the student. When service-learning is integrated into the curriculum, it provides structured time for students to think, reflect, and learn (National and Community Service Act of 1990). Service-learning also is seen as a belief system about how education works and what we can do in — and out — of the classroom (MacNichol, 1993).

Service-learning is partly an educational methodology, partly a philosophy of learning, and partly a developmental strategy for schools and communities (Cairn, 1992). Students learn through active participation in thoughtfully organized experiences and use newly acquired skills in meaningful life situations (National and Community Service Act of 1990). Moreover, service-learning is a highly sensible instructional strategy in that it involves youth as important community resources (Council of Chief State School Officers, 1993) and in planning their own learning experiences. Service-learning truly is "something old" and "something new" since it is based on John Dewey's notion of learning-by-doing and on the modern constructivists' perspective that knowledge is actively built when learners are adequately challenged to find meaning in their actions. Service-learning, as many observers indicate, is based on action, reflection, and analytical thinking about the experiences. Lastly, service-learning is seen as a means of assessing learning (Cairn, 1992) in that it takes what students should know and what they should be able to do and, most importantly, uses it to make schools and communities better places in which to live and work (Kielsmeier, 1992).

Administrative roles and responsibilities   To be successful, service-learning requires continuing guidance and supervision of well-trained administrators, teachers, and community members (Alliance for Service-Learning in Education Reform, 1995). Administrators provide the leadership and support needed to transform the culture of schools, since isolated teachers, no matter how effective they are, cannot mobilize the resources needed to "make it happen."

Policymaking and policy alignment   Many states are developing service-learning initiatives consistent with Anderson's (1993) perspective that systemic educational reform policies support high standards for students, learning and achievement, alternative assessment, and flexible instruction; with Fuhrman and Massell's (1992) perspective that unprecedented efforts are being undertaken to integrate policies; with Smith and O'Day's (1991) perspective that policy components are being tied to standards; and with Sashkin and Egermeier's (1993) perspective that state education policies are attempting to provide coherent structures to support schools in designing strategies for teaching the content of the emerging curriculum frameworks.

A Brief Summary

For service-learning to be a lasting part of systemic educational reform, it must be viewed as a philosophy, a process, and an instructional strategy rather than an interrupting or intrusive program or project. As a method of teaching and learning, service-learning provides real purposes and audiences for learning, an excellent entry point to learning styles, and opportunities to apply academic concepts through experience and reflection. Service-learning should never become a burden that teachers are forced to incorporate into their professional responsibilities.

In summary, here are 12 major principles:

- "It" is based on policy and program alignment.
- "It" is standards based and standards driven.
- "It" connects schools with other social systems and community groups.
- "It" is based on school/community networks and partnerships.
- "It" is intended to build respect and tolerance for all.
- "It" is aimed at improving the school's culture and governance structure.
- "It" is aimed at developing higher-order thinking, decision-making, and problem-solving skills.
- "It" is based on the application of knowledge in real-world situations.
- "It" seeks to integrate curriculum, instruction, and assessment.
- "It" attempts to integrate academic and applied learnings throughout the curriculum.
- "It" seeks to develop lifelong learners actively engaged in their learning both in and out of the classroom.
- "It" is built on authentic ways of ascertaining what students know and can do.

The "it" to which we are referring is, of course, both service-learning and systemic educational reform. Both concepts are based on these 12 principles.

Martin Luther King, Jr., once said, "Everyone can be great, because everyone can serve." Everyone, indeed, can serve — and learn. Children and youth who traditionally have been viewed as passive consumers can become active contributors. Those served in the past can become servers. Service-learning can be a way of recapturing the idealism of the 1960s but with "value added," that is, with a strong learning component complementing an equally strong service ethic. But whether a service-learning culture permeates schools and communities or remains on the fringes of the educational reform agenda is still unknown. Its considerable potential for educational revitalization, however, is beyond question.

Part III

References
and Appendices

Part III

References

Alliance for Service-Learning in Education Reform. "Standards of Quality for School-Based Service-Learning." *Equity & Excellence in Education* 26.2 (1993): 71–73.

—. *Standards of Quality for School-Based and Community-Based Service-Learning.* Washington, DC: Council of Chief State School Officers, 1995.

Anderson, B.L. "The Stages of Systemic Change." *Educational Leadership* 51.1 (1993): 14–17.

Anderson, J. D. "Leave School and Learn: Seekonk High School's Independent Study Program." *Equity & Excellence in Education* 26.2 (1993): 30–34.

Anderson, V., C. Kinsley, P. Negroni, and C. Price. "Community Service Learning and School Improvement in Springfield, Massachusetts." *Phi Delta Kappan* 72.10 (1991): 761–764.

Armstrong, P. M. *Community Studies and Service Program — San Francisco School Volunteers: Final Program Evaluation Report, Academic Years 1988–89 through 1991–92.* Alameda, CA: Organizational DATA, 1992.

Armstrong, P. M., and A. B. Crowe. *Community Studies and Service Program: Second Semester Brief Evaluation Report.* Alameda, CA: Organizational DATA, 1990.

Association for Supervision and Curriculum Development. "Learning through Service." *ASCD Update* August 1993.

Barber, B.R. "A Mandate for Liberty." *Visions of Service: The Future of the National and Community Service Act.* Eds. S. Sagawa and S. Halperin. Washington, DC: National Women's Law Center and American Youth Policy Forum, 1993.

Benard, B. *Youth Service: From Youth as Problems to Youth as Resources.* OSAP Workshop on Youth Involvement, 1990.

Bhaerman, R. D. *Integrating Education, Health, and Social Services in Rural Communities: Service Integration through the Rural Prism.* Philadelphia, PA: Research for Better Schools, Inc., 1994.

Boyte, H. C. "Community Service and Civic Education." *Phi Delta Kappan.* 72.10 (1991): 765–767.

Briscoe, J. "Citizenship, Service, and School Reform in Pennsylvania." *Phi Delta Kappan.* 72.10 (1991): 758–760.

Brown, C. E. "Caring as an Educational Experience." *Equity & Excellence in Education.* 26.2 (1993): 18–21.

Cairn, R. "Another Way of Learning." *The Generator* Spring 1992.

Carnegie Council on Adolescent Development. *Turning Points: Preparing American Youth for the 21st Century.* New York: Carnegie Corporation of New York, 1990.

Clark, T. "National and Community Service: Strengthening the Next Phase." *Visions of Service: The Future of the National and Community Service Act.* Eds. S. Sagawa and S. Halperin. Washington, DC: National Women's Law Center and American Youth Policy Forum, 1993.

Conrad, D., and D. Hedin. *High School Community Service: A Review of Research and Programs.* Madison, WI: National Center on Effective Secondary Schools, 1989.

Constitutional Rights Foundation. *A Planning Conference on School-Based Service.* Los Angeles, CA: Constitutional Rights Foundation, 1992a.

——. *Behind the Sciences: Curriculum Concepts.* Los Angeles, CA: Constitutional Rights Foundation, 1992b.

——. *Reflection and Community Service.* Los Angeles, CA: Constitutional Rights Foundation, 1992c.

——. *60 Minute Community Search.* Los Angeles, CA: Constitutional Rights Foundation, 1992d.

——. *Starting Off Right with Teachers and Administrators.* Los Angeles, CA: Constitutional Rights Foundation, 1992e.

Corporation for National and Community Service. *National and Community Service Trust Act of 1993: A Summary.* Washington, DC: Corporation for National and Community Service, 1993.

Council of Chief State School Officers. *Concerns* July 1993.

——. *Concerns* October 1994.

——. "Connecting School-to-Work Career Initiatives and Service Learning." *Concerns* August 1996.

——. *Integrating Service Learning into Teacher Education: Why and How?* Washington, DC: Council of Chief State School Officers, 1995.

——. Memorandum on *Connecting Goals 2000: Educate America Act and Service Learning.* Washington, DC: Service Learning Project of the CCSSO, n.d.

——. *Summary of the 7/22/94 Discussion and Examples of Service-Learning Models with a School-to-Work Focus.* Washington, DC: Council of Chief State School Officers, 1994.

—. *The Service Learning Planning and Resource Guide.* Washington, DC: Council of Chief State School Officers, 1994.

Dirks, F. "The Challenge of Community Building." *Visions of Service: The Future of the National and Community Service Act.* Eds. S. Sagawa and S. Halperin. Washington, DC: National Women's Law Center and American Youth Policy Forum, 1993.

Duckenfield, M., and L. Swanson. *Service-Learning: Meeting the Needs of Youth at Risk.* Clemson, SC: National Dropout Prevention Center, 1992.

Ellis, B. C. "Using CSL with Special Education and Reading Resource Students." *Equity& Excellence in Education* 26.2 (1993): 15–17.

Fertman, C. I. *Service Learning for All Students.* Bloomington, IN: Phi Delta Kappa Educational Foundation, 1994.

Follman J., J. Watkins, and D. Wilkes. *Learning by Serving: 2,000 Ideas for Service-Learning Projects.* Greensboro, NC: SouthEastern Regional Vision for Education, 1994.

Fuhrman, S., and D. Massell. *Issues and Strategies in Systemic Reform.* CPRE Research Report Series RR-025. New Brunswick, NJ: Consortium For Policy Research in Education, October 1992.

Gomez, B. "How the National and Community Service Act Can Help Advance Education Reform." *Visions of Service: The Future of the National and Community Service Act.* Eds. S. Sagawa and S. Halperin. Washington, DC: National Women's Law Center and American Youth Policy Forum, 1993.

Gonzalez, J., F. W. Wagner, and D. Brunton. "Community Service Learning at Putman High School." *Equity & Excellence in Education.* 26.2 (1993): 27–29.

Haberman, M. The Top 10 Fantasies of School Reformers. *Phi Delta Kappan.* 75.9 (1994): 689–692.

Halperin, S. "Youth Service Is Also about Changing Adults." *Visions of Service: The Future of the National and Community Service Act.* Eds. S. Sagawa and S. Halperin. Washington, DC: National Women's Law Center and American Youth Policy Forum, 1993.

Hamilton, S. F., and M. A. Hamilton. *Opening Career Paths for Youth: What Can Be Done? Who Can Do It?* Washington, DC: American Youth Policy Forum, 1994.

Hedin, D., and D. Conrad. "Service: A Pathway to Knowledge." *Community Education Journal.* 51.1 (1987): 10–14.

Hillman, C. *Service Learning, a Key to Rural Regeneration.* Harrisburg, PA: Pennsylvania Institute for Environmental and Community Service Learning, n.d.

Honnet, E. P., and S. J. Poulsen. *Principles of Good Practice for Combining Service and Learning.* Wingspread Special Report. Racine, WI: The Johnson Foundation, Inc., 1989.

Hoyt, K. B. "Career Education and Transition from Schooling-to-Employment." *Youth Policy.* 15 & 16.12 & 1 (1994): 10–19.

Jobs for the Future. *Learning that Works: A School-to-Work Briefing Book.* Boston, MA: Jobs for the Future, 1994.

Kazis, R. *Improving the Transition from School to Work in the United States.* Washington, DC: American Youth Policy Forum, Competitiveness Policy Council, and Jobs for the Future, 1993.

Kelliher, M. F. "Community Service Learning: One School's Story." *Equity & Excellence in Education.* 26.2 (1993): 12–14.

Kendall, J. C., and Associates. *Combining Service and Learning: A Resource Book for Community and Public Service.* Vol. 2. Raleigh, NC: National Society for Internships and Experiential Education, 1990.

Kennedy, E. M. "National Service and Education for Citizenship." *Phi Delta Kappan.* 72.10 (1991): 771–773.

Kielsmeier, J. "Reflections: Doing, Knowing, and Being." *The Generator* Spring 1992.

Kingsland, S. F., M. Richards, and L. Coleman. *A Status Report for KIDSNET, Year One, 1994–1995.* Portland, ME: University of Southern Maine, 1995.

Kinsley, C. W. "Community Service Learning as a Pedagogy. *Equity & Excellence in Education.* 26.2 (1993): 53–59.

Kurth-Schai, R. "The Roles of Youth in Society: A Reconceptualization." *Educational Forum.* 52.2 (1988): 113–132.

Loesch-Griffin, D.,and T. Lobman. *Breaking Even: Cycles of Support and Suffering.* Reno, NV: Turning Point, Inc., 1993.

Loesch-Griffin, D., L. A. Petrides, and C. Pratt. *A Comprehensive Study of Project YES — Rethinking Classrooms and Community: Service-Learning as Educational Reform.* CA: East Bay Conservation Corps, 1995.

MacNichol, R. "Service Leaning: A Challenge to Do the Right Thing." *Equity & Excellence in Education.* 26.2 (1993): 9–11.

Maryland State Department of Education. *Student Service Learning: Involving Voluntary Student Organizations.* Baltimore, MD: Maryland State Department of Education, n.d.

Maryland Student Service Alliance. *Spinning Interdisciplinary Service-Learning Webs: A Secondary Education Approach.* Baltimore, MD: Maryland State Department of Education, 1995.

McPherson, K. "Project Service Leadership: School Service Projects in Washington State." *Phi Delta Kappan.* 72.10 (1991): 750–753.

Mendel, R. *The American School-to-Career Movement: A Background Paper for Policymakers and Foundation Officers*. Washington, DC: American Youth Policy Forum, 1994.

Miller, B. "Service-Learning in Support of Rural Community Development." National Service-Learning Conference. Philadelphia, PA. 8 March 1995.

Nathan, J., and J. Kielsmeier. "The Sleeping Giant of School Reform." *Phi Delta Kappan*. 72.10 (1991): 739–742.

Northwest Regional Educational Laboratory. "Bringing a Sense of Connection to the Community." *Northwest Policy* May-June 1994.

O'Day, J. A., and M. S. Smith. "Systemic Reform and Educational Opportunity." *Designing Coherent Education Policy: Improving the System*. Ed. S. H. Fuhrman. San Francisco, CA: Jossey-Bass Publishers, 1993.

Orenstein, H. "A Legislator's Case for Service-Learning." *The Generator* Spring 1992.

Ouellette, G. "Documenting Learning through Service: Cognitive and Affective Growth in a Service-Learning Program." *The Generator*. Spring 1992.

Parsons, C. "It's a Worrisome Thing . . ." *Visions of Service: The Future of the National and Community Service Act*. Eds. S. Sagawa and S. Halperin. Washington, DC: National Women's Law Center and American Youth Policy Forum, 1993a.

—. *Removing Barriers: Service Learning in Rural Areas*. Washington, DC: Council of Chief State School Officers, 1993b.

—. "SerVermont: The Little Initiative that Could." *Phi Delta Kappan*. 72.10 (1991): 768–770.

Perrone, V. "Learning for Life: When Do We Begin?" *Equity & Excellence in Education*. 26.2 (1993): 5–8.

Portner, J. "At Your Service." *Education Week*. 23 November 1994: 19+.

Sagawa, S. "Historical Background: An Overview." *Visions of Service: The Future of the National and Community Service Act*. Eds. S. Sagawa and S. Halperin. Washington, DC: National Women's Law Center and American Youth Policy Forum, 1993.

Sashkin, M., and J. Egermeier. *School Change Models and Processes: A Review and Synthesis of Research and Practice*. Washington, DC: U.S. Department of Education, 1993.

Sausjord, I. "Research on Children, Youth, and Prejudice: Some Implications for Service Learning." *CRF Network* Fall 1993.

Schine, J. "Incentives for High Quality in Service-Learning." *Visions of Service: The Future of the National and Community Service Act*. Eds. S.

Sagawa and S. Halperin. Washington, DC: National Women's Law Center and American Youth Policy Forum, 1993.

—. *Young Adolescents and Community Service.* Washington, DC: Carnegie Council on Adolescent Development, 1989.

Seidman, A., and C. Tremper. *Legal Issues for Service-Learning Programs.* Washington, DC: Nonprofit Risk Management Center, 1994.

Seigel, S., and V. Rockwood. "Democratic Education, Student Empowerment, and Community Service: Theory and Practice." *Equity & Excellence in Education.* 26.2 (1993): 65–70.

Senate Bill 676. *Service Learning Act of 1993.* Washington, DC: 103d Congress, 1st Session, 1993.

Shaffer, B. *Service-Learning: An Academic Methodology.* Stanford, CA: Stanford University, Department of Education, 1993.

Shumer, R. *Executive Summary — Describing Service-Learning: A Delphi Study.* St. Paul, MN: University of Minnesota, 1993.

Smilow, P. "How Would You Like to Visit a Nursing Home?" *Equity & Excellence in Education.* 26.2 (1993): 22–26.

Smith, M. S., and J. O'Day. "Systemic School Reform." *The Policies of Curriculum and Testing.* Eds. S. H. Fuhrman and B. Malen. New York: Falmer Press. 1991.

South Carolina Department of Education. *Serving to Learn: High School Manual.* Columbia, SC: South Carolina Department of Education, 1994.

Supple, C. J. "Youth Service and Education Reform." *The Generator* Spring 1992.

Townsend, K. K. "Making Service-Learning the Center of the Debate on School Reform." *Visions of Service: The Future of the National and Community Service Act.* Eds. S. Sagawa and S. Halperin. Washington, DC: National Women's Law Center and American Youth Policy Forum, 1993.

vonGlasersfeld, E. "Questions and Answers about Radical Constructivision." *The Practice of Constructivism in Science Education.* Ed. K. Tobin. Washington, DC: AAAS Press, 1993.

Wutzdorff, A. "Moving in from the Margins." *Visions of Service: The Future of the National and Community Service Act.* Eds. S. Sagawa and S. Halperin. Washington, DC: National Women's Law Center and American Youth Policy Forum, 1993.

Part III

Appendix A
. . . .

Principles, Standards, Steps

Along the Way, and Guideposts

Teachers and administrators do not have to start at "ground zero" in order to transform a school's culture to include service-learning. A number of principles, standards, "steps along the way," and guideposts have been developed for establishing quality initiatives.

Principles

The 10 Principles of Good Practice in Combining Service and Learning were written by Honnet and Poulsen (1989) and resulted from extensive consultations conducted by the National Society for Internships and Experiential Education (now NSEE) with more than 70 organizations interested in service and learning. These principles should be considered in the context of particular local needs and purposes. We have abbreviated them here; for a more detailed account, readers are urged to read Honnet and Poulsen's full report in which they provide numerous examples that indicate where each principle is being addressed programmatically throughout the country. Copies of the full report can be obtained from the Johnson Foundation, or by contacting the National Society for Experiential Education, 3509 Haworth Drive, Suite 207, Raleigh, NC 27609.

Honnet and Poulsen contend that an effective initiative adheres to these principles.

(1) (It) *engages people in responsible and challenging actions for the common good*. Participants engage in tasks they and the community recognize as important. These tasks require moving beyond one's range of previous experience. Active participation requires accountability for one's actions, involves the right to take risks, and gives participants opportunities to experience the consequences of those actions for themselves and others.

(2) (It) *provides structured opportunities for people to reflect critically on their service experience*. Experiences alone do not insure that significant learning or effective service will occur. Initiatives must provide

. . . .

opportunities for participants to think about what they have learned. Through reflection, participants can develop an enhanced sense of social responsibility. Reflection is most useful when it is continued throughout the experience and when feedback is provided from the persons being served as well as from peers.

(3) (It) *articulates clear service and learning goals for everyone involved.* Both participants and recipients must have a sense of what is to be accomplished and learned. Both service and learning goals must be agreed on and should reflect the input of those providing as well as receiving services.

(4) (It) *allows for persons with needs to define those needs.* Recipients of service must have a role in defining their service needs. Community service programs, government agencies, and private organizations can be helpful in defining what tasks are needed and how they should be performed. Such collaboration will insure that services will not take jobs away from the community but rather that it involves tasks that otherwise would not be conducted.

(5) (It) *clarifies the responsibilities of each person and organization.* Several parties — students, teachers, supervisors, and sponsoring organizations as well as individuals and groups receiving services — are involved in any effort. It is important to clarify roles and responsibilities; the process includes identifying and assigning responsibilities and acknowledging the values important to all of those involved.

(6) (It) *matches service providers and service needs through a process that recognizes changing circumstances.* Since people often are changed by the experience, initiatives must build in opportunities for feedback about the changing needs of those involved. Participation affects personal development in such areas as intellect, cross-cultural understanding, and empathy. In effective initiatives, although relationships among groups and individuals are dynamic, they also may create dilemmas that may lead to unintended outcomes.

(7) (It) *expects genuine, active, and sustained organizational commitment.* Initiatives must have ongoing commitment from both the sponsoring and receiving organizations. Commitments can take many forms, including references to service-learning in the organization's mission statement. The initiatives must receive administrative support; become budget items; be allocated appropriate space, equipment, and transportation; and allow for adequate time for everyone involved. In schools, service-learning must be linked to the curriculum and require that the faculty become committed to it as a valid part of teaching.

(8)   (It) *includes training, supervision, monitoring, support, recognition, and evaluation.* Effective efforts are sensitive to the importance of training, supervision, and monitoring progress. A reciprocal responsibility requires communication between those offering and those receiving services. Both the sponsoring and receiving organizations should recognize the value of service through appropriate celebrations and public acknowledgment of individual and group service. Also, planned, formal, and ongoing evaluation should be part of every effort.

(9)   (It) *insures that the time commitment for service and learning is flexible, appropriate, and in the best interests of all involved.* Some activities require longer participation and/or greater time commitment that others. The length of the experience and the amount of time required are determined by the tasks involved. An activity can do more harm than good if it is abandoned after too short a time or given too little attention.

(10) (It) *is committed to program participation by and with diverse populations.* Effective strategies promote access and remove barriers to participation. Persons responsible for these initiatives should make every effort to include people from different ethnic, racial, and religious backgrounds, as well as people of varied ages, genders, economic levels, and disabilities. The need for sensitivity to such barriers as lack of transportation; family, work, and school responsibilities; concern for personal safety; and uncertainty about one's ability to make a contribution are extremely important.

Standards

The Alliance for Service-Learning in Education Reform is a national coalition of organizations and individuals from educational, youth development, and youth leadership agencies that advocates the integration of service-learning into K–12 education as method of instruction and educational philosophy. One of its priorities is high-quality practice through well-articulated standards. The Alliance for Service-Learning in Education Reform (1995) has developed a comprehensive set of standards of quality for school-based and community-based service-learning. The following is an abbreviated overview of the standards. For a more detailed account, readers are urged to review the March 1995 standards publication of the Alliance. For more information, contact Dr. Barbara Gomez, Council of Chief State School Officers, One Massachusetts Avenue, NW, Suite 700, Washington, DC 20001.

(1)   *Effective service-learning efforts strengthen service and academic learning.* Efforts should begin with clearly stated goals to be achieved

through structured preparation, reflection, and the service itself. Learning goals (knowledge, skills, attitudes) must be compatible with the students' developmental levels.

(2) *Model service-learning provides concrete opportunities for youth to learn new skills, think critically, and test new roles in an environment which encourages risk taking and rewards competence.* Service experiences are not ends in themselves. By performing meaningful service, young people can develop new skills and try different roles, thus reinforcing connections between the world inside and outside of the classroom.

(3) *Preparation and reflection are essential elements in service-learning.* These two elements give service-learning its educational integrity. Preparatory study of underlying problems and policies enriches learning, as do discussion and other classroom activities. Preparation should introduce skills and attitudes needed for effective service. Reflection is the framework in which students process and synthesize the information and insights they have gained. Through it, they analyze concepts, evaluate experiences, and form opinions — all in the context of the curriculum.

(4) *Youths' efforts will be recognized by those served, including their peers, the school, and the community.* During the service as well as in a culminating event, students should share with the community what has been gained and given through service. Recognizing the work that students perform reinforces the significance of the enterprise and the worth of young people.

(5) *Youth are involved in the planning.* When young people are given the opportunity to serve, they are entrusted with the expectation that they have the ability to serve. Since building trust is essential to the success of the effort, it is critical to involve young people from the beginning. This approach provides teachers with opportunities to foster planning and analytical skills.

(6) *The service students perform makes a meaningful contribution to the community.* Projects that involve students differ, depending on the students' age, the learner's goals, and the community's needs. Whatever the activity, services must be real, must fill a recognized need, must be developmentally appropriate, and should result in a tangible outcome or product that, when possible, demonstrates the learning outcomes.

(7) *Effective service-learning integrates systematic, formative, and summative evaluation.* Although anecdotal evidence is useful, systematic methods for assessing impact also are needed. Such assessments should include documentation of all of the components and processes as well as the outcomes identified by, and expected of, all

of the participants. Assessments vary in extent and complexity, depending on the questions asked and the available time and resources. A combination of formative assessment (to inform practice) and summative assessment (to evaluate impact) helps ensure that the initiatives remain responsive to their purposes and participants.

(8) *Service-learning connects the school or sponsoring development organization and its community in new and positive ways.* Service-learning has the potential of reducing barriers that may separate the school and community.

(9) *Service-learning is understood and supported as an integral element in the life of a school or sponsoring organization and its community.* For service-learning to succeed, it must receive support for both its philosophy and financial requirements. Both school-based and community-based initiatives must have the support of the district and building administrators and community institutions.

(10) *Skilled adult guidance and supervision are essential to the success of service-learning.* Effective service-learning requires the guidance and supervision of well-trained teachers, administrators, and community members.

(11) *Pre-service training, orientation, and staff development that include the philosophy and methodology of service-learning will best ensure that program quality and continuity are maintained.* Teacher education programs should include service-learning instruction; potential teachers should be involved in service-learning as part of their pre-service preparation.

Steps Along the Way

In addition to the general principles and standards, various steps have been suggested for those who wish to develop service-learning initiatives. Kinsley (1993) describes this five-step developmental process: (1) involving students and other stakeholders; (2) identifying a need in the school or community; (3) establishing a theme; (4) connecting with community partners; and (5) determining objectives and organizing the learning experiences.

Shaffer (1993) presents a seven-step approach: (1) establishing a school or classroom theme; (2) determining objectives; (3) selecting content (identifying major ideas to be learned, reviewing academic areas applicable to the theme, selecting specific content for each grade); (4) selecting and organizing learning experiences (determining how you can involve the following in the experience: reading, writing, observation, research, problem solving, discussion, art, music, and drama): identifying what information and skills students are expected to learn and what outcomes are expected; building a repertoire of activities; developing learning experiences; meeting with community representatives; and establishing timelines; (5) orienting students; (6) performing the service; and (7) reflecting on the experience.

Kelliher (1993) identifies eight steps: (1) identifying needs; (2) contacting community agencies; (3) enlisting help by asking those who have a particular skill that is needed; (4) choosing realistic deadlines; (5) making instructions clear and easy to follow; (6) publicizing the activity; (7) following up with thank-you notes or an appreciation gathering; and (8) reflecting — the most important step — by asking students these questions: How has the service benefited you? How has it changed your attitude? What did you learn?

Whether it is five, seven, eight, or more steps, action planning is essential for developing quality service-learning initiatives.

Guideposts

The service-learning knowledge base is growing rapidly. A countless number of "helpful hints" exists, many of which are based on the observations of practitioners who, in some cases, have been involved with service-learning for more than a decade. An attempt to extract the essence of their insights has been made by compiling a brief list of several important "guideposts" or guidelines. Perhaps the most important one is that there is no one single approach. It is not a matter of finding the correct "model" to adopt or adapt as it is finding the proper "mix" of what is needed and what realistically can be provided.

Beginning early Service-learning can be developed with a view toward reducing prejudice as early as the pre-school level. Primary school students have had successful experience with senior citizens of different ethnic backgrounds. Assigning upper elementary school students to develop oral histories also has been successful. Both the National Association for the Education of Young Children and the Anti-Defamation League offer materials with age-integrated with service experiences (Sausjord, 1993).

Conducting a "60 minute" community search Students often do not have to travel long distances to perform service. One activity that has been suggested by the Constitutional Rights Foundation (1992) is to conduct a "60 minute" search in which groups of elementary students obtain a map of the school and draw a one-mile radius around it. Groups of three to five students then "search" the community as part of a homework assignment. For one hour, each team records parks that may need cleaning, walls that need to be free of graffiti, businesses that might sponsor group efforts, and other potential community participants. More extensive "city searches" are described by the Constitutional Rights Foundation for older students in which "issue teams" are formed to interview persons in different segments of city life. This activity is followed by debriefings with the entire class to determine prospects for service-learning. Students and teachers develop a "Rolodex mentality" of chronicling what is going on in their communities and how they may be of service.

Conducting an awareness conference In order to gain the commitment of teachers, the Constitutional Rights Foundation (1992) recommends an awareness and planning conference that introduces key concepts for effective initiatives and provides incentives for ongoing development. The Foundation describes such a conference conducted in Pasadena: Much needed to be done before that conference, e.g., establishing a representative committee to develop the agenda, identifying resource persons, and preparing resource materials. After the conference, feedback was provided prior to the next step, i.e., acting on recommendations.

Conducting needs assessments One of the first steps in developing service-learning involves assessing the needs of the community as well as the interests of potential participants. Duckenfield and Swanson (1992) suggest that it is critical that students be involved in identifying community problems and social issues. They can research community agencies, interview community activists, and conduct surveys and site visits to witness problems first hand. After gathering the needed background information, they can then select the areas in which they will serve, depending on the available time and resources.

Encouraging team efforts Sausjord (1993) recommends team efforts with the groups structured for diversity. She also suggests ensuring that each person has a well-defined and essential task. Where teams work together over a period of time, rotating roles helps ensure equal status and responsibility within the group.

Evaluating progress The Maryland State Department of Education (n.d.) has developed useful evaluation guideposts. They suggest several guiding questions that should be considered (e.g., Were the objectives met? In what areas did they fall short? What did the participants learn? What services were performed? And were the services valuable to the recipients?). Much of the information needed to answer these and similar questions can be derived from a journal kept by all participants.

Developing inter-group relations It is important to encourage students to consider making issues of inter-group relations, race, ethnicity, and prejudice a primary focus (Sausjord, 1993). Sausjord also suggests that setting up a weekend exchange project in which Latino, African American, and Anglo-American students visit each other's homes has a powerful impact on the students providing service.

Developing skills Certain skills need to be acquired before actual participation, e.g., such general service skills as cooperation, communication, organization, responsibility, problem solving, and awareness of working with special populations. The service also may require that participants learn specific techniques through hands-on experience, e.g., learning how to take water samples, performing Cardio-Pulmonary Resuscitation, or learning the correct way to push a wheelchair (Duckenfield and Swanson, 1992).

Involving youth in program governance Youth involvement affects the success of service-learning by encouraging fresh ideas, building initiatives that reflect the interest of young people, and increasing their accountability to themselves as well as to the adults with whom they work. The Constitutional Rights Foundation (1992) suggests involving youth as members of governing boards, advisory boards, and/or leadership teams. They also suggest conducting youth training activities prior to program involvement, e.g., training in committee work, budgeting, and developing group unity.

Planning for action The Maryland State Department of Education (n.d.) suggests several important action-planning questions: What will be done to achieve the desired outcomes? Who will do what? What individual and group assignments need to be made? What resources are needed? What resource people are needed to teach skills? What will it cost? How will it be financed? What is the time schedule? How will it be promoted and publicized? From what support groups and/or individuals will assistance be sought? And will follow-up activities be conducted to ensure that the plan is carried out?

Preparing students It is important to prepare students before calling on them to work with people of different backgrounds. Sausjord (1993) suggests that teachers begin by assessing students' readiness by providing, as appropriate, activities designed to correct misinformation and stereotypes and by helping students examine their own attitudes. Inviting members of the community to speak to the class can be a worthwhile start. Appropriate reading and role playing also can help students develop empathy for others.

Recognizing the effort It is important to celebrate and publicize activities and promote the "good news." The Maryland State Education Department (n.d.) suggests using school and local newspapers, radio, TV, and other media to inform the public about the benefits of service-learning.

Thinking critically The emphasis should be on critical thinking during all stages of the activity. Students of all ages should be encouraged to develop opinions on community issues and proposed solutions. When students voice opinions (as they should be encouraged to do), teachers should follow up with questions that explore how students arrived at the opinion and on what evidence they relied. Sausjord (1993) proposes that, in addressing the goal of developing "cognitive sophistication," students should investigate and analyze community problems first, examine alternatives next, and — only after in-depth critical thinking — decide on a service-learning initiative to address the issues.

Part ■■■

Appendix B
· — · · · · · · · · · · · · · · · ·

Selected Curriculum Guides

Albert, G., and the Staff of the University of Vermont Center for Service-Learning. *Service-Learning Reader: Reflections and Perspectives on Service.* Raleigh, NC: National Society for Experiential Education, 1994.

Cairn, R. W. *Learning by Giving: K–8 Service-Learning Curriculum Guide.* St. Paul, MN: National Youth Leadership Council, 1993.

Cairn, R. W., and J. C. Kielsmeier. *A Sourcebook on Integrating Youth Service into the School Curriculum.* Roseville, MN: National Youth Leadership Council, 1991.

Conrad, D., and D. Hedin. *High School Community Service: A Review of Research and Programs.* Madison, WI: University of Wisconsin, National Center on Effective Secondary Schools, 1989.

Conrad, D., and D. Hedin. *Youth Service: A Guidebook for Developing and Operating Effective Programs.* Washington, DC: Independent Sector, 1987.

Council of Chief State School Officers. *The Service Learning Planning and Resource Guide.* Washington, DC: Council of Chief State School Officers, 1994.

Gulati-Partee, G., and W. Finger. *Critical Issues in K–12 Service-Learning: Case Studies and Reflections.* Raleigh, NC: National Society for Experiential Education, 1996.

Henderson, K. *What Would We Do Without You? A Guide to Volunteer Activities for Kids* Crozet, VA: Shoe Tree Press, 1990.

Kendall, J. and Associates. *Combining Service and Learning: A Resource Book for Community and Public Service.* Volumes 1 and 2. Raleigh, NC: National Society for Internships and Experiential Education, 1990.

Klosterman, G. *Guides to Developing Service-Learning Programs.* St. Paul, MN: National Service-Learning Cooperative, University of Minnesota, 1996.

Lewis, B. *The Kid's Guide to Service Projects — Over 500 Service Ideas for Young People Who Want to Make a Difference.* Minneapolis, MN: Free Spirit Publishing, Inc., 1995.

—. *The Kid's Guide to Social Action: How to Solve the Social Problems You Choose — and Turn Creative Thinking into Positive Action.* Minneapolis, MN: Free Spirit Publishing, Inc., 1991.

Maryland State Department of Education. *High School Service-Learning Guide.* Baltimore, MD: Maryland State Department of Education, 1993.

National Society for Internships and Experiential Education. *Service-Learning: An Annotated Bibliography.* Raleigh, NC: National Society for Internships and Experiential Education, 1988.

Salzman, M., and T. Reisgies. *150 Ways Teens Can Make a Difference: A Handbook for Action.* Princeton, NJ: Peterson's Guides, Inc., 1991.

Sckukar, R., J. Johnson, and L. R. Singleton. *Service Learning in the Middle School Curriculum: A Resource Book.* Boulder, CO: Social Science Education Consortium, 1990.

Silcox, H. *A How-to Guide to Reflection: Adding Cognitive Learning to Community Service Programs.* Holland, PA: Brighton Press, Inc., 1993.

Witmer, J. T., and C. S. & Anderson. *How to Establish a High School Service Learning Program.* Alexandria, VA: Association for Supervision and Curriculum Development, 1994.

Zimmerman, R. *What Can I Do to Make a Difference? A Positive Action Source Book.* New York, NY: Penguin Books, 1991.

Part ■■■

Appendix C
· ·

Resource Organizations

Association of Experiential Education, 2885 Aurora Avenue, #28, Boulder, CO 80303-2252

Close-Up Foundation 44 Canal Center Plaza, Alexandria, VA 22314

Community Service Learning Center, 333 Bridge Street, Suite 8, Springfield, MA 01108-1419

Community Service Learning Program, Lincoln Filene Center, Tufts University, Medford MA 02155

Constitutional Rights Foundation, 601 South Kinglsey Drive, Los Angeles, CA 90005

Corporation for National and Community Service, Learn and Service America Programs, 1201 New York Avenue, NW, Washington, DC 20525

Council of Chief State School Officers, One Massachusetts Avenue, NW, Suite 700, Washington, DC 20001-1431

Institute for Service Learning, Philadelphia College of Textiles and Science, Henry Avenue and School House Lane, Philadelphia, PA

National Association of Partners in Education, 209 Madison Street, Alexandria, VA 22314

National Dropout Prevention Center, Clemson University, Clemson, SC 29634-5111

National Helpers Network, Inc., 255 Fifth Avenue, Suite 1705, New York, NY 10016-8761

National Service Learning Clearinghouse, University of Minnesota, 1954 Buford Avenue, St. Paul, MN 55108-6197

National Society for Experiential Education, 3509 Haworth Drive, Suite 207, Raleigh, NC 27609

National Youth Leadership Council, 1910 West County Road B, St. Paul, MN 55113-1337

Project Service Leadership, 12703 NW Avenue, Vancouver WA 98685

RMC Research Corporation, 1521 Larimer Street, Suite 540, Denver, CO 80202

Service-Learning Research and Development Center, Graduate School of Education, University of California at Berkeley, 2223 Fulton Street, Fourth Floor, Berkeley, CA 94720

Quest International, 537 Jones Road, P.O. Box 566, Granville, OH 43023-2700

· ·

Part III

Appendix D
. . . .

Resource Centers and Clearinghouses

National Resource Center
for Experiential and Service Learning

National Society for Experiential Education, 3509 Haworth Drive, Suite 207, Raleigh, NC 27609-7229, (919) 787-3263, fax (919) 787-3381, nsee@netstart.net.

NSEE's National Resource Center for Experiential and Service Learning houses and disseminates information on hundreds of topics related to experiential education and programs that combine service and learning. The goal of the Resource Center is to provide resources related to the theory and practice of experiential education in order to assist in the professional development of members and non-members and to be responsive to the needs of the field. The Resource Center contains information created by and for practitioners and also serves as a vehicle for resource sharing — encouraging members and non-members to share materials they have developed that would be helpful or informative to others in the field. These resources, collected since 1978, contain published and unpublished books, articles, manuals, papers, conference materials, and video and audio cassette tapes that cover:
- program design and administration;
- research;
- theory and rationale; and
- course materials.

The Resource Center is housed at NSEE headquarters in Raleigh, North Carolina. Anyone seeking information can make an appointment to visit the Resource Center and use the computerized index to locate information. It is also possible to submit a Resource Center Request Form to obtain a personalized packet of materials. A packet consists of:
- a bibliography of published materials, and
- up to 10 pages of unpublished materials, and/or
- referrals to NSEE members or to other organizations.

K–12 Clearinghouse on Service-Learning

National Service-Learning Cooperative, 1-800-808-SERVE, National Information Center for Service-Learning, R-290 Vo-Tech Building, 1954 Buford Avenue, St. Paul, MN 55108, (612) 625-6276, fax (612) 625-6277.

The National Youth Leadership Council, along with major collaboration from the University of Minnesota, is cooperating with numerous other universities and organizations around the country to develop a Clearinghouse for information and technical assistance on service-learning. Funded by the Commission on National and Community Service, the initial goal of the Clearinghouse is to assist Serve-America grantees and help educators and community agencies develop and expand service-learning opportunities for all youth. The Clearinghouse provides many services. Staff can provide you with information on the following:

* The Serve-America program, including legislation program operation, state contacts, special services provided by the Corporation for National and Community Service, and other details about the federal effort to promote service-learning;

* Organizations engaged in promoting service-learning and community service;

* Model programs around the country which exemplify the best practices of service-learning;

* Databases around the country dealing with youth service, youth development, youth at-risk, dropout prevention, youth employment, and other topics related to the entire service-learning field; and

* National calendar of conferences and training opportunities related to service learning.

In addition, the Clearinghouse provides:

* Information about programs and curricula for the major forms of service-learning;

* Bibliographies and literature on service-learning;

* Names and phone numbers of people who provide technical assistance on all aspects of service-learning; and

* The NSLC Gopher Server containing service-learning related information which is accessible through the Internet.

Part III

Appendix E
∙∙

State Education Agency
Service-Learning Contacts

Alabama State Department of Education
50 North Ripley Street
Montgomery, AL 36130-3901
(334) 242-8059   (334) 242-0482 FAX

Director
Comprehensive Training Unit
Division of Vocational and Technological Education
Arizona Department of Education
1535 West Jefferson
Phoenix, AZ 85007
(602) 542-2037   (602) 542-1849 FAX

Administrative Adviser
Arkansas Department of Education
4 Capitol Mall, Room 405-B
Little Rock, AR 72201
(501) 682-4399   (501) 682-4618 FAX

Learn & Serve Coordinator
ICYSD-CalServe, 3rd Floor
721 Capitol Mall
P.O. Box 944272
Sacramento, CA 94244-2720
(916) 657-5442   (916) 657-4969 FAX

Director, Service-Learning
Co-Director, Middle Grade School State Policy Initiative
Colorado Department of Education
201 East Colfax Avenue
Denver, CO 80203-1705
(303) 866-6897   (303) 830-0793 FAX

NOTE: Most states have developed service-learning training, curriculum, and resource materials

Service Learning Coordinator
Connecticut Department of Education
165 Capitol Avenue
Hartford, CT 06106
(203) 566-1961   (203) 566-2957 FAX

Gifted and Talented Programs
Department of Public Instruction
Box 1402, Townsend Building
Dover, DE 19903-1402
(302) 739-4667   (302) 739-4483 FAX

Rabaut Administration Building
2nd & Peabody Street, NW
Washington, DC 20011
(202) 541-5928   (202) 541-5918 FAX

Learn and Serve
Florida State University
Center for Civic Education & Service
930 West Park Avenue
Tallahassee, FL 32306-2059
(904) 644-3174   (904) 644-3362 FAX

School Support Services Unit
State Department of Education
1762 Twin Towers East
Atlanta, GA 30334
(404) 657-8335   (404) 651-8984 FAX

Instructional Services
189 Lunalilo Home Road, 2nd Floor
Honolulu, HI 96825
(808) 396-2505   (808) 548-5390 FAX

Coordinator, Chapter 2 Programs
Len B. Jordan Office Building
650 West State Street
Boise, ID 83720
(208) 334-2186   (208) 334-2228 FAX

Coordinator of Special Programs
Illinois Resource Center
1855 Mt. Prospect Road
Des Plaines, IL 60018
(708) 803-3535   (708) 803-3342 FAX

Consultant
Service Learning and School Restructuring
Center For School Improvement and Performance
Indiana Department of Education
Room 229, State House
Indianapolis, IN 46204-2798
(317) 233-3163   (317) 232-9121 FAX

Director
Iowa Center For Community Education
Iowa Department of Education
Grimes State Office Building
Des Moines, IA 50319-0146
(515) 281-3290   (515) 242-6025 FAX

Learning Specialist
Kansas Department of Education
P.O. Box 889
Topeka, KS 66601
(913) 234-1423   (913) 234-1429 FAX

Consultant
Student/Family Support Services
Kentucky Department of Education
500 Mero Street
Capitol Plaza Tower, Room 1711
Frankfort, KY 40601
(502) 564-3678   (502) 564-6952 FAX

Director Learn & Serve America
1051 N Third Street, #321
Baton Rouge, LA 70802
(504) 342-2038   (504) 342-1218 FAX

Serve America Grant Coordinator
Department of Education
State House Station #23
Augusta, ME 04333
(207) 287-5923   (207) 287-5927 FAX

Maryland Student Service Alliance
Maryland State Department of Education
200 W. Baltimore Street
Baltimore, MD 21201
(410) 767-0364   (410) 333-2379 FAX

Co-Coordinator
Community Service Learning Program
Instruction and Curriculum Services
Department of Education
350 Main Street
Malden, MA 02148-5023
(617) 388-3300 ext. 272   (617) 388-3395 FAX

Serve Michigan Coordinator
Michigan Department of Education
P.O. Box 30008
Lansing, MI 48909
(517) 373-8863   (517) 373-3325 FAX

Youth Development and Youth Services
Minnesota Department of Children, Families, & Learning
550 Cedar Street
St. Paul, MN 55101
(612) 297-2481   (612) 296- 3348 FAX

Serve America Coordinator
Office of Deputy Superintendent
Mississippi Department of Education
P.O. Box 771
Jackson, MS 39205
(601) 359-3602   (601) 359-2326 FAX

Learn and Serve Supervisor
Dept. of Elementary & Secondary Education
400 Dix Road
Jefferson City, MO 65109
(573) 526-5395   (573) 526-3897 FAX

Service-Learning Director
P.O. Box 202501
Montana Department of Education
Helena, MT 59620
(406) 444-5726

Director
Nebraska Serve America
Nebraska Department of Education
P.O. Box 94987
301 Centennial Mall South
Lincoln, NE 68509-4987
(402) 471-4812   (402) 471-0117 FAX

Community Service Grant Manager
Nevada Department of Education
Capitol Complex
700 East 5th Street
Carson City, NV 89710
(702) 687-3136   (702) 687-5660 FAX

Learn and Serve Consultant
New Hampshire Department of Education
101 Pleasant Street
Concord, NH 03301
(603) 271-3719   (603) 271-1953 FAX

Learn and Serve Program
Office of Innovative Programs
Division of Academic Program and Standards
Department of Education
100 Riverview Plaza
CN 500
Trenton, NJ 08625
(609) 633-8014   (609) 633-9825 FAX

New Mexico Department of Education
Learn and Serve Liaison
300 Don Gaspar Street
Education Building
Santa Fe, NM 87501
(505) 827-4055   (505) 827-4041 FAX

Bureau Chief
Liberty Partnership Program Administration
New York State Education Department
Cultural Education Center, Room 5C84
Empire State Plaza
Albany, NY 12230
(518) 486-5202   (518) 474-0060 FAX

North Carolina Department of Public Instruction
Division of Communication Services
301 North Wilmington
Raleigh, NC 27601-2825
(919) 715-1242   (919) 715-1021 FAX

Project Manager
Serve-America
Center For Teaching and Learning
University of North Dakota
Box 7189
Grand Forks, ND 58202
(701) 777-2675   (701) 777-4393 FAX

Serve America Grants Coordinator
Room 1009
65 Front Street
Columbus, OH 43085-4087
(614) 466-8920   (614) 728-3058 FAX

Oklahoma Serve-America Program
Coordinator
Oklahoma State Department of Education
2500 North Lincoln Boulevard
Oklahoma City, OK 73105
(405) 521-4795   (405) 521-6205 FAX

Volunteer Development Coordinator
Oregon Department of Education
255 Capitol Street, N.E.
Salem, OR 97310-0203
(503) 378-8142   (503) 373-7968 FAX

Learn and Serve Coordinator
Pennsylvania Department of Education
333 Market Street
Harrisburg, PA 17126-0333
(717) 783-9290   (717) 793-6617 FAX

Rhode Island Department of Elementary and Secondary Education
The Shepard Building
255 Westminster Street
Providence, RI 02903-3400
(401) 277-6523   (401) 277-4979 FAX

South Carolina Department of Education
1429 Senate Street, Room 906
Rutledge Building
Columbia, SC 29201
(803) 734-8071   (803) 734-5685 FAX

Director
School Age Child Care and Special Projects
State Department of Education
6th Floor, Gateway Plaza
710 James Robertson Parkway
Nashville, TN 37243-0375
(615) 741-0345   (615) 741-6236 FAX

Director
ServeAmerica Program
Region 14
Education Service Center
1850 Highway 351
Abilene, TX 79601
(915) 675-8640   (915) 675-8659 FAX

Education Specialist
Utah State Office of Education
250 East 500 South
Salt Lake City, UT 84111
(801) 538-7826   (801) 538-7882 FAX

Service Learning Coordinator
School Development and Information Team
Vermont Department of Education
120 State Street
Montpelier, VT 05602
(802) 828-5405   (802) 828-3146 FAX

Educational Studies
Oliver Hall-South
1015 West Main Street
P.O. Box 842020
Richmond, VA 23284-2020
(804) 828-1323

Program Supervisor
Serve America
Superintendent of Public Instruction
Old Capitol Building
P.O. Box 47200
Olympia, WA 98504-7200
(360) 753-3302   (360) 664-3575 FAX

Department of Education
1900 Kanawha Blvd East, Building 6
Room B-221
Charleston, WV 25305
(304) 558-2348   (304) 558- 3946 FAX

Consultant For School Administration
School and Community Relations
Wisconsin Department of Public Instruction
P.O. Box 7841
125 S. Webster Street
Madison, WI 53707-7841
(608) 266-3569   (608) 267-1052 FAX

Wyoming Department of Education
2300 Capitol Avenue
Hathaway Building, 2nd Floor
Cheyenne, WY 82002-0050
(307) 777-6198   (307) 777-6234 FAX

Part ■■■

. . . .

Services and Publications

of the National Society for

Experiential Education

The National Society for Experiential Education is a nonprofit member-ship association and national resource center that promotes the use of learning through experience for:

- academic development
- civic and social responsibility
- career exploration
- cross-cultural awareness
- leadership development
- ethical development

NSEE's mission is to foster the effective use of experience as an integral part of education, in order to empower learners and promote the common good. Founded in 1971, NSEE assists schools, colleges, universities, and organizations in the field of experiential education, which includes:

- school-to-work
- service-learning
- internships
- field studies
- study abroad programs
- cooperative education
- leadership development programs
- practicum experiences
- active learning in the classroom

NSEE publishes the *NSEE Quarterly*, resource papers, monographs, and books, including:

- *Combining Service and Learning: A Resource Book for Community and Public Service*
- *Critical Issues in K–12 Service-Learning: Case Studies and Reflections*
- *Service-Learning Reader: Reflections and Perspectives on Service*

- *Research Agenda for Combining Service and Learning in the 1990s*
- *The National Directory of Internships*
- *The Experienced Hand: A Student Manual for Making the Most of an Internship*
- *The Internship as Partnership: A Handbook for Campus-Based Coordinators & Advisors*
- *The Internship as Partnership: A Handbook for Host Agencies & Site Supervisors*
- *Strengthening Experiential Education within Your Institution*
- *Legal Issues in Experiential Education*
- *Origins and Implications of the AmeriCorps National Service Program*

and other publications covering issues of Practice and Application, Rationale and Theory, and Research

NSEE's National Resource Center for Experiential and Service Learning provides information and referrals on the design and administration of experiential education programs, policy issues, research, and more. NSEE sponsors national and regional conferences and offers consulting services for those wishing to strengthen experiential education within their institution.

Benefits of NSEE membership include:

- a subscription to the *NSEE Quarterly — to keep you informed on innovations in the field*
- substantial discounts on publications, annual conference registration, consulting, and NSEE Resource Center materials — *to give you the tools you need for improved practice*
- opportunities to join Special Interest Groups and Networks — *to connect you with colleagues across the country*
- opportunities to participate in special projects — *to test new experiential learning approaches*
- full voting privileges as well as eligibility for election or appointment to the NSEE Board of Directors — *to exercise leadership in the organization and the field*

For more information or to become a member, contact NSEE:

3509 Haworth Drive, Suite 207   Raleigh, NC 27609

919/787-3263 PHONE   919/787-3381 FAX
nsee@netstart.net E-MAIL   http://www.tripod.com/nsee INTERNET

Dr. Robert D. Bhaerman is currently the Project Associate in the Consortium on Inclusive Schooling Practices at the National Association of School Boards of Education in Alexandria, Virginia. Previously, he was Director of Public Policy, Legislation, and Communications at the Quality Education for Minorities (QEM) Network in Washington, D.C. He has also served as a senior research and development specialist at both Research for Better Schools, the former regional education laboratory for the mid-Atlantic states, and the National Center for Research in Vocational Education when the Center was located at The Ohio State University. He has published widely in the area of school-to-work transition and, more recently, on the concept of integrating education, health, and social services.

Dr. Karin M. Cordell is the Director of the Curriculum Branch for the District of Columbia Public Schools. Previously, she served as an Education Associate in Curriculum Frameworks and Standards at the Delaware Department of Public Instruction. She has also been a training coordinator and educational specialist at COMSIS, the mid-Atlantic Multi-functional Resource Center and has worked as a consultant in the areas of bilingual and multicultural education. She has taught at elementary, secondary, and university levels, and has worked as a counselor and psychologist.

Barbara Gomez is the Director of the Service-Learning Project at the Council of Chief State School Officers (CCSSO). She also serves as a consultant to the Corporation for National Service for K–12 Learn and Serve programs. Previously, she has worked as a field researcher for a national welfare reform research study, a manpower development specialist with the U.S. Department of Labor, an independent consultant on youth employment and training programs, a career planning and placement counselor at a major California university, a junior high school teacher, and a school/community liaison. She has published in the areas of integrating service-learning into educational reform and connecting service-learning and school-to-careers.